W9-BFO-596

KING, WARRIOR, MAGICIAN,

WEENIE

CONTEMPORARY MEN'S HUMOR
EDITED BY PETER SINCLAIR

THE CROSSING PRESS, FREEDOM, CA 95019

Deepest thanks to my father for his support during this project. To my wife Sandy, for teaching me patience. To my children, Brendan and Shaylyn, for teaching me to love. To Britt Eustis and Ann Sinclair for prodding me at a critical moment. To my mother for teaching me persistence. To Keir Todd and John Price for being sounding boards, and to Bob Thibodeau and Mary Wolf for teaching me about timing.

Copyright © 1993 by Peter Sinclair
Cover Design by Mott Jordan
Cover Illustrations by Peter Sinclair
Interior Design by Amy Sibiga
Printed in the U.S.A.

Library of Congress Cataloging in Publication Data
King, warrior, magician, weenie. contemporary men's humor / edited by
   Peter Sinclair.
         p.   cm.
      A collection of cartoons, essays, and poems.
      ISBN 0-89594-646-7 (cloth). -- ISBN 0-89594-595-9 (paper)
      1. Men--Humor. 2. Masculinity (Psychology)--Humor. 3. Men-
-Caricatures and cartoons. I. Sinclair, Peter.
PN6231.M45K56 1993
817'.54080352041--dc20
                                                    93-5340
                                                    CIP

table of contents

iNtroductioN

Let me say first of all that this book is primarily aimed at being funny. Humor is a rare and precious commodity these days (the proliferation of cable comedy specials just proves my point). Let me also say this book has been put together by people who like the men's movement, understand it, and support it. Who, to coin a phrase, "get it."

A lot of people still don't think men need their consciousness raised. After all, men still get paid more, grab the plum jobs, the big deals, the corner office. If they happen to kill themselves four times as often as women, well, isn't that what being a man is all about? Live large, go for it, no regrets, pump yourself up, stiff upper lip, twisted steel and sex appeal, lean, hard, cut, and ripped to shreds, suck it up, go down with the ship, fall on the sword, die hard. What's wrong with this picture?

Think about the last time you were at the doctor's office surreptitiously thumbing through those pamphlets about breast self-exams? When is the last time you did a testicular self-exam? Hey, guys, it's a major killer of young men. Or didn't you know? Women have been getting to know their bodies and themselves for 25 years. So where are we?

And then there's the one that goes, "The Men's Movement? That's for middle-age, middle-class, white guys with time on their hands." Right. So take a survey of your local poor, Black, Hispanic, or Asian gang members and ask them about their deep and soulful relationship with their fathers.

Part of the problem is journalists, or what I call the "secular humorless establishment." The mytho-poetic men's movement is fundamentally about spirit, the unconscious, the deeper dimension. This makes journalists uneasy. They are, after all, the same dweebs who did your yearbook in high school. Spirit was something you raised at pep rallies. Ten or 20 years later, this geeky credulity takes its revenge by dumping questions of soul into the flake category, or better yet, the "new age," "woo, woo" dust bin.

The real men's movement is practical and down to earth. In putting this book together I didn't look for stuff about guys drumming in the woods (although we have that), so much as just anything reflecting the peculiarities of guyhood in general. Men and women, men and work, men and family, men and dogs, fathers and sons, men and TV, men and beer, men and sports, men and other men.

We need a movement to illuminate the little corners of post-industrial manhood. We need to awaken Kings, Warriors, Lovers, and Magicians. But we desperately need the Trickster as well, to deflate us and keep us honest. When you're dealing with pain, humor makes it bearable. It's the only anesthetic that clears the head, sharpens the mind, and awakens the senses. And science now tells us that humor is a peerless healer.

I'm convinced that in time science will also show that, 20 years of feminist recrimination notwithstanding, testosterone, when used properly (sipped and savored, not chugged, Rambo style) is like fine red wine, a boon and balm to all personkind.

I've collected all styles of humor here, and it cuts in many directions. Something (I hope) to make everyone laugh a little, and (I hope) something to get just a little under everyone's skin. Remember now, it's a joke! Relax. You're with your buddies. In the schoolyard. In the locker room. On the floor around a fire. "Two guys walk into a bar . . ."

Does it hit a little close to home? Gotcha! Two points! Psych! I get noogies.

Peter Sinclair
Midland, Michigan

Studly Warrior Stuff

real men don't... don't do what?

BY LEWIS GRIZZARD

The other day I read an article about a Conference on Men and Masculinity. I think it is a grand idea to hold such a thing.

Over the past couples of decades, a lot of men have had to ask themselves a lot of tough questions about masculinity, such as, "Should I keep wearing boxer shorts or switch to bikini briefs?" and, "Should I get some curtains for this place?"

Masculinity used to be a simple thing to define. If you had hair on your chest, a deep voice, and belonged to a club that excluded women, you were masculine, or, as was the phrase of the time, "a man's man."

But all that changed. The feminist movement came along, and suddenly women were saying they preferred Phil Donahue over Charles Bronson.

It was okay to be sensitive. It was okay to cry.

Dennis the Menace took down the sign on his tree house that read NO GIRLS ALLOWED and welcomed Margaret inside.

Men's fashion rules changed. It was okay to wear pink. Then it was okay to wear an earring. Then it was okay for a man to wear his hair with a ponytail in the back.

But the new rules of masculinity, as I mentioned before, confused a lot of men, especially men my age, those who don't have enough hair left to make a ponytail in the first place and who are hurtling toward prostate trouble.

We learned masculinity from our fathers, our scoutmasters, and our high school coaches—veterans of World War II, stand-up guys who were against long hair and drank their beer from a bottle.

Our heroes were John Wayne and Aldo Ray. If Phil Donahue had been in our school, we would have beaten him up on the playground.

But look at us now, we are trying to fit in. Do we stay with Old Spice or switch to something with a name like "Dark Musk"?

Do we use mousse (something we used to hunt) on our hair? Should we order a glass of white wine or stick with Budweiser? Should we discuss football when we are bonding, or the crisis in funding for the arts?

I overheard a comment made by a male friend the other day that is quite telling.

He's mid-forties, and he said, "I'm just glad my father didn't live long enough to see me playing golf with my wife on Saturdays and getting my hair cut in a beauty parlor."

As for my personal beliefs concerning masculinity, I have become more tolerant in the past years.

I have at least two male friends who have ponytails. One also wears an earring. They are still my good friends. I never ask them over to watch a tape of *Sands of Iwo Jima*, but they are still good friends.

I get my own hair cut where it's coed. I allow the waiter to pour my beer in a glass. I have a male friend who has a cat. I've stopped questioning his masculinity.

I believe women deserve equal pay with men. I read articles by women sportswriters. I don't believe there was ever a woman raped who was asking for it.

But I still wear boxer shorts, and the first time Margaret said, "You really should be getting some curtains for this place," it would be the last time she saw the inside of my tree house.

I haven't come that far, baby.

robert bly

BY IAN SHOALES

Robert Bly was a poet who could
Dream it would do guys some good
If they banged on a drum
'Till their fingers were numb
With some other guys out in the wood.

Frankly, Manly Men, it's time for us to get ugly

BY FRANKLIN CRAWFORD

I just finished listening to a Robert Bly tape. Those of you who don't know about Robert Bly have been spared a great deal of bad poetry, and I shan't destroy your pristine ignorance by quoting any lines.

Anyway, it's Bly's current campaign to make real men out of the American male that has grabbed my attention. I think he's on to something.

Bly has become a mentor to audiences full of naive, nearing middle-aged American men who have been beaten into submission by—first, he points out—the Industrial Revolution, and (much) later, the Feminist Movement. He goes around the country doing workshops for men. Bill Moyers interviewed him in a PBC special called "A Gathering of Men" not long ago. The show opened with the white-haired poet slapping a Native American rhythm on a drum, his impossible jaw ajut as he told an audience full of pale, vulnerable-looking guys a strange tale about men who disappeared in a wood near a castle…

Right, I was feeling a little queasy too.

But I had to admit that this white old man was saying something important. He went on to talk about what he called The Naive Male: the guy who just doesn't know what's happening and keeps getting kicked by the same horse time and again. The horse is, usually, a mare.

I see dozens of such men each day. I might even be one myself, but that's confidential and I trust you won't tell anybody, because if it gets around that I'm a sissy, geez, girls will giggle in their shirtsleeves when I walk by and I might have to start cooking at home.

What captured my imagination was Bly's description of the contemporary "soft man," the New Age fella who's tried so hard to be sensitive he doesn't know how to ask for what he wants anymore. The way I see it, this soft guy has given his power over to his wife or lover and can't get it back. Look at him: He's changing the baby's diapers, he's reading *Our Bodies Ourselves* while on the toilet, he's asking Her if it's OK for him to drink beer and watch some football. He's washed his hands, cleaned his ears, his fingernails, and he's made sure his breath doesn't smell. He brings home the Tofu, he's a sourdough breadwinner. He wants Her to be happy. He's a good guy.

What's he get? His wife leaves him for a tattooed sleaze on a Harley who drinks Old Milwaukee and farts a lot.

Well, something like that, anyway.

How did these soft guys turn into such ziplock bags full of worm guts? Bly thinks the roots of wimphood lie in the Industrial Revolution and the introduction of the daytime job.

> but i had to admit that this white old man was saying something important.

"The Grind", as it has become known through history, took Daddy out of the house and left potential Napoleons home with Mommy where they stayed long after puberty, eating curds and whey and getting too comfy to want to go out and conquer the world. Sons only knew their fathers as grouchy, dangerous men who smelled like beer when they came home from work, long after suppertime. From their hiding places behind the ice box, young bucks listened to their parents argue sluggishly in the dark, and the dysfunctional family was born. Would-be Solomons cringed with embarrassment while Daddy bellowed obscenities and Mommy calmly sliced him to bits with clever responses, the way women will when they are confronted with an irrational man.

Bly doesn't bother saying what was happening to the daughters during this time. That's what I like about about him.

Anyway, Bly says, a wounded image of the Father has emerged, American men are suffering grief, he postulates, because we haven't been properly initiated into manhood; because there aren't any decent Male Mentors out there (he's right, you know—a quick breeze through recent heroes produces Reagan, Batman—close second to Bill Murray in *The Ghostbusters*—and Michael Jackson. OK OK, Richard Dysart, too); because young men hate old men and old men don't care about young men's souls anymore; because nobody asked young men if they wanted to be circumcised or not: and mostly because we hung around mom too long. We're hurting.

But who we gonna call?

Bly suggests the Wildman, that nasty bottom dweller who's been supping on pond scum in the deep recesses of our primal beings, just waiting for a chance to show his stuff. He's an ugly brute, but fear him not, ladies, he's the man for whom you've been waiting.

Oh, manly men, do you not see yourselves in these teachings?

Once he unites with the vulnerable, sensitive fellow you created yourselves with your damned Feminist diatribes against the evils of the male ego—you're gonna swoon.

Why? Look at it this way. Out of touch with the Wildman inside of him who not only gets the job done, but doesn't take any guff while he's doing it, today's "soft male" has become a sly, mealy-mouthed shadow, afraid to tell his girlfriend he doesn't like her earrings for fear she'll leave him. Then he creates a situation whereby he becomes so repulsive she has to leave him and then he feels OK because it was *her fault*. He joins a support group, moans a lot, then finds a sweet, dependent honeybunch who he can later betray.

Oh, manly men, do you not see yourselves in these teachings?

I once swore that if anybody ever tried to get me to go to some Men's Potluck Dinner and Discussion about manhood, I'd kick their butts for them—for their own good.

But the terrible truth is that I too have been a-nipping on Mother's Milk long after the expiration date. I've been avoiding that terrible confrontation with the booga-booga man who's been making bubbles in the deep, reeking cesspit of my subconscious.

So, I'm getting me a bongo drum. I'm growing a beard. I'm gonna stop taking showers. I'm gonna slaver like a stallion on steroids and snarl like a rabid dog. I'm gonna tell dirty stories that'll curl your nose hairs and come two weeks from now...

I'll be writing in jail.

Charles Atlas Shrugged:
the unbearable Lightness of being Male

BY ROBERT A. SIDES

We are all journeymen, returning to ourselves. We seek renewed meaning to our lives. We shun traditional roles, which had all the joy and spontaneity of Burma Death Marches. Instead, we follow the yellow bliss road to Oz. We want high adventure, not low lives of quiet desperation. We quest inward and out, alone and together, for a better, brighter Big Picture.

Too often, though, we forget that Bigness, like God, is in the details. We forget that significance can be found in small things. Sometimes the tiny makes the trivial terrifying. Indiana Jones botches a theft and so must haul kiester to outrun Paul Bunyan's bowling ball. Other times the minute makes the mundane momentous. Young, frustrated Clark Kent hurls a "useless" crystal, and presto! He raises the glorious glacial Fortress-of-Solitude. Who'da thunk it? Fate's like that, fickle. It goes where it will, like wildmen seeking wisdom.

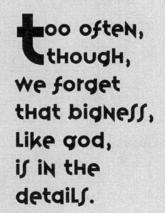

too often, though, we forget that bigness, Like god, is in the details.

But in which direction? To what larger purpose?

So I asked, having read an article on randy teens. (I am, after all, a firm, nay tumescent, believer in life-long sex education. And, ahem, practice.) Events began predictably enough. First, a young feminnocent posed the standard query: should she surrender her pudendal pearl-of-great-price to a swinish swain? "Nevermore!" Quoth the craven Ms. Lowen Lee-Hartz, sin-dictated columnist and dyspeptic dispenser of duenna-isms. The usual answer. Nothing new there, standard unfair-to-men fare. The eternal, maternal marching orders were issued: Beauty must forever defend against the beasts (er, boyfriends). Ever it was thus.

The next tale, however, was different. Its small question had great consequences for me. Would the effects be for the better or worse? Now or forever? Simply or profoundly? Out, out, damned answers! (Read on, Macduffs!)

A young boy, whose scrotum no tote'em them manly follicles, told his sorry story. Bathroom bullies, seeing his inscrutable un-hirsute-able sack, had dubbed him "Baldy." Saddled with such a moniker, what could our hero do? His plea was Proust's Madeleine to me, a remembrance of un-macho things past. Back, back I went, on my un-sentimental journey to . . .

My first, wet communion Bashful baptism, or trial by water? You tell me. The crime scene? The much-maligned men's locker-room. Used to solitary ablutions at home (yep, a once-a-month bath, needed or not), I was suddenly forced to communally scrub. Herded together, we dirty-dozen boys got no dry run, no pre-shower peptalk. We were unceremoniously dumped beneath spritzing nozzles, nekkid as the day we wuz born. Awkward and scared, we looked like plucked chickens doing the Acid Bath Dance. Still, we were properly-trained pumped-up premen. Group showers were no harder than, say, pooping in public. At Yankee Stadium. In the middle of the infield. With bleachers full. And bases loaded.

Outwardly we were cool, Jule. But inwardly? Brothers, we wuz dyin'!

Did we towel-off and talk of our angst? Did we stare at each other? Did we cry us a river? (Did Mighty Casey hit a homer?) Noooooo! We knew the cardinal rule of Casa Macho, like the cosa nostra, was omertà: silence! (And *"Oh merde,"* "Oh, shit!"—for any broken silence.) Ours was not to listen why; ours was but to do…and sigh, out of sight. Adversity was met with song: "Happy travails to you, until we meet (and compete) again . . ." Roger that, Roy!

In short, the first shower casualty was shyness. Then modesty. Then truth. No one said Eddie was hung like a horse ("Mr. Ed," indeed!); that Mike's back looked like someone'd put a fire out on it with an ice-pick; that several of us were still unwilling members of the Baldini Brotherhood (we few, we unhappy hairless few!). We knew to keep our traps shut. We'd mastered the disdain-pain game. We knew the penalties, for crying out loud, so we didn't. We broke neither silence nor wind (well, no more than usual). We'd stoically withstood the Rain of Terror. We knew the girls would, too.

Not for the last time would sexism raise its ugly head.

The lasses, alas, had separate, individual, curtained showers. It was another blow to the wedge driving us apart. First there'd been their inability to pee their names legibly in the snow, or aim directly at cigarette butts in toilet-bowl battles of "Sink The Bismarck." Then their growing pref-

erence for hopscotch, dolls, and the color pink over infinitely more interesting frogs, mud and spit. Lately some had even toned down their belches. It was, as the King of Siam said, a puzzlement. Still, by and large, we wuz still buddies.

Imagine our shock, then, when no feminine protest arose over such sexist showers! Imagine our further dismay hearing girls tell their coach, Ms. Buldike, that they needed privacy . . . because it was "that time of the month." What? Had they forgotten how to lie now, too? If they wanted to duck class—an honorable motive, surely—why use such a lame excuse? I mean, who'd buy it? It's always some time of the month, right? And what'd that have to do with anything anyway?

The girls were starting to act as dumb as the folks we'd read about in English class. A colonial preacher said he'd taken the governor's wife into the woods and knew her. So? Of course he "knew" her: they'd met in Church, right? And of course it was "biblically," since they'd read the Bible together. Big fussing deal! Who cares? Yet, the congregation went bonkers, and so did the girls in our English class. They, too, became a mob, whispering and giggling like a bunch of . . . girls. They were gettin' strange.

Things got stranger.

For Catholics, Confirmation is the drafting of Christian soldiers into the army of the Lord. For boys, it was a sacred and scarey rite. It meant taking "The Slap." See, weenies weren't allowed in God's wars. So his main recruiter, Bishop Brimstone, had to tape our cheeks to test our spiritual mettle. It symbolized the torture we'd smilingly endure when the Commies took over. Hey, no problema.

Not for the last time did reality raise its howling head.

Outwardly we were cool, Jule. But inwardly? Brothers, we wuz dyin'!

On the big day, Sister Mary Knucklewhacker allowed that the Slap might be more than a tap. Under no circumstance, however, were we to flinch. Concern etched our cherubic faces. We boys, seated separately, were the first to face the holy music (as ever, first into danger, last into lifeboats). We queued to prove our manhood. Pete led the charge, kneeling before Christ's proxy. A gun fired. Pete's head recoiled. Then Joe knelt. Another shot fired. Recoil. Tom knelt. "Kapow!" Suddenly, Pete passed back through our ranks, returning to his pew. We beheld a pale walker. He was devoid of color, save for a big bright-red handprint on his cheek. Uh, oh: Big Problema! Those weren't gun shots, those were the slaps! Our Bjorn-again Bishop, it seems, was using our cheeks as tennis balls in his match with Satan.

One question shot through Mr. Roger's now-shaking neighborhood: can you spell . . . LETSGETTHE-HELLOUTTAHERE?

It was quite a spectacle. And not just because Wally ducked, permitting the Bishop to display his formidable backhand. No, the most memorable thing was our keen (and now red-faced) anticipation of the next event—the slaughter of our co-lambs, the girls. We barely contained our glee. Not one of us proto-men had broken. Neither peeps, nor peed pants stained our honor. Now a thousand girly-girl cries would fill the air. Forty days and nights of tears would fall. Equality was at bat. Awriiiiiiight!

Judy was on deck. Alice approached the plate, er, guillotine, er, Bishop. Smiles beamed from our be-crimson'd faces. The next sound would be sweet. You could hear an angel-topped pin drop. His Holiness wound up. His pastoral pitch was released. Yesssssss! We held our breath. Thank you, Jeeeeesus! Then . . . nothing. Zilch. Silencio. Nada. Alice quietly regained her pew. No scarlet hand tattooed her pious face. What the?

Not for the last time was inequality savored by the girls.

Turns out the Bishop, the fink, was a gender-specific Jeremiah. He kaboshed the boys, coddled the girls. Jesus's only hope now was if the Reds rustled Eddie, not Carole. The Ed-sel could smite them with his courage, faith, and equestrian appendage. Carole could but muster cooties and tears.

More burdens piled atop our boyish backs.

Remember school-yard fights? Girls had some, but they were tepid affairs. Ours were heroics, imaginative, majestic. Many were the duels-to-death I fought . . . in daydreams. I rescued fair maidens Lucy, Pam and Barbara this way. And often after school I'd don Superman's cape (mom's dish-towel) and jump off hills formed by new-house excavations. Titanic king-of-the-hill battles were waged against pretenders to my/ Supe's throne. Dirt "bombs" provided ready ammo. B-movie Greek god extravaganzas taught tactics. Steve Reeve's Hercules inspired my skill-at-arms. Upstart Macedonians, cleverly disguised as garbage cans, felt the wrath of Jove's javelins (Dad's beanpoles). War was hell, but only on my clothes. Mostly it was great fun.

Then Jimmy showed his ugly face for the first and last time.

Something there is that hates a fat lip. No one wants one. The threat of getting one ruins regularity of one's day and peristalsis. The sooner the threat is heard, the longer the former seems, the looser the latter becomes. So it was with me and Jimbo. My school day was spent in a frenzy of alliance-making, lest I faced the entire James Gang alone. I couldn't eat. I couldn't think. My heart beat like Big Ben bonged by King-Kong-turned-Krupa. Then it was high noon. I tried walking tall toward Un-gentle-man Jim, but was no Gary Cooper. I felt I was climbing the gallows with an ice-cube up my butt. I was fear. But I didn't show it, so Jimmy-the-Geek didn't know it.

The "Fight of the Century" lasted 3 minutes. Mutual head-locks ruled it a draw. The gasping gladiators respectfully declined a re-match.

I had, as they say, no heart for fightin'. Luckily, my battles were few, tame, and far between. Fear could eat my adrenalin like Roseanne Barr at an all-you-can-eat buffet. I dreaded boyish bashings and couldn't wait to begin the peace process. Today, when even water pistols lead to death, I'd never make it. Knives, guns, and Mace have replaced puerile pugilism and recreational wrasslin'. Walk softly now, and you're still hit with a big stick.

Anyway, I ineluctably grew into high school. There I meet the "hoods." No, not neighbor-HOODs, but HOODlums. Given my fierce fighting dispirit, I quickly became adept at avoiding/befriending them. I mastered these arts by the process of elimination. Well, during it, really. See, the turf of the hoods was the Men's Room. There they smoked butts, and on occasion kicked some. To dissuade the former and preclude the latter, the administration removed all stall doors. The result would've daunted then-reigning, bullet-disdaining, lead-spewing hero, Sir John Rooster-Cogburn Wayne. Could "The Duke" have used the loo in full view of a motley crew? The sands of Iwo Jima were nothing by comparison. It took true grit to simply sit and, er, deliver. Excretion without discretion is tyranny!

Which raises other questions in the gland scheme of things:

• If it's good for Scouts to help old ladies cross streets, why is it bad for them to "help" Mother Nature exercise Master Bation? And are "nocturnal emissions" just smokestack pollutants released at night?

• Why does tile grout become so fascinating when we face it, standing at public urinals?

• Have you ever aimed "Mr. Happy" so his torrent announces to all pee peers present, "Let no man think I stand here idly playing pocket-pool!"?

• Who painstakingly rubs those peepholes through solid stone stall-walls, the Count of Monty Crisco? How long does he take? Does he have a day job? Does he really expect someone to "Stick it in here"? Does he wait on the other side, ready to tie Mr. Happy in a Gordian knot? Or bonk it with a 50-pound sledgehammer?

• Didja ever slip off your boyhood bike pedal, feel that familiar bone-and-boner-bashing "zing!" and say "Enough is enough! I'm swapping my crotch-crusher for a safer, bar-less, better designed girl's model?" NOT!

• Didja ever consider enhancing your man-root with a homemade Penisizer ("Bend and tie one end of short rope to cinder block. Tie other to Mr. Unhappy. Now, slowly stand up . . . ")?

• Was Eddie's favorite description of his Proud Pestle "A Baby's Arm Holding An Apple," or "Yul Brynner Wearing A Turtleneck With a Hatchet Mark On His Head"?

Well, me buckos, we made it to manhood, more or less. We learned to drive cars, smoke cigars, and bear our scars. We loved and lost and lived to love again. We had sand kicked in our faces and feet put other places. We paid our dues.

It's not been easy; never was a cake-walk. And I, for one, am tired of hearing it was. We're no collection of callous, uncaring kings. We're serfs who've shouldered burdens Atlas shrugged off. Now it's time men, too, threw off sex-role chains. Let's lighten the load, free our souls, put fun back into fatherhood and family. Let's take one small step for feelings, one giant step toward self-fulfillment.

And woe to those who try to stop us. We'll heed the counsel of philosopher-kings Moe, Larry, and Curly. If we meet any guilt-mongering, male-bashing, frenzied feminazis blocking our path, why we oughta . . .

But that's another story. For now, my merry macho muchachos, it's back to the future: "Presennnnnnt Bean-poles!" Macedonian garbage cans march against us.

TOM the DANCING BUG

WHEN THEIR DIVERSE PERSONALITIES AND TALENTS ARE BROUGHT TOGETHER, THEY CAN DO THE **IMPOSSIBLE!!**
THEY'RE-- **THE IMPOSSIBLE SQUAD!**   ©1991 ROOTIN' RUBEN BOLLING

SGT. MAC HARDY
DOUBLE-FISTED, NAILS-
EATING POWERHOUSE!
SPECIALTY: EXPLOSIVES

SGT. ROCK RUMBLE
BARREL-CHESTED, HOT-
HEADED TOUGH GUY!
SPECIALTY: EXPLOSIVES

SGT. NICK WYLDE
HARD-NOSED, GUTSY
DOUBLE-FLUSHER!
SPECIALTY: EXPLOSIVES

SGT. KURT STEELE
HEAVYWEIGHT, FISTS
FLYIN' HOT SHOT!
SPECIALTY: EXPLOSIVES

SGT. JACK DUKES
CIGAR-CHOMPING,
HULKING STEAMROLLER!
SPECIALTY: ENTOMOLOGY

OKAY, YOU PALOOKAS, LISTEN UP! HERE'S THE MISSION: WE GOTTA TAKE OUT THIS SUPPLY BRIDGE! ANY BRIGHT IDEAS?

I SAY WE GO WIT' EXPLOSIVES! LET'S BLOW THAT SUCKER TO *PEORIA!!*

YEAH, THAT LOUSY BRIDGE AIN'T NOTHIN' SOME GOOD OL' *TNT* CAN'T HANDLE!

YEAH!

NOW, HOLD YER STOGIES!! I GOT A BETTER IDEA! I SAY WE USE...

TERMITES!!

AW, DUKES! NOT AGAIN...!

SURE! WE JUST LET A FEW THOUSAND *ISOPTERAS* LOOSE AND WATCH THE FUN! IN A FEW MONTHS, THOSE BABIES...

THAT DOES IT, DUKES!! I'VE HAD IT WIT' YER BLASTED BUGS! IT'S ALWAYS **ANTS** THIS, AN' **BEES** THAT! I'M GONNA SQUASH YOU FER GOOD!!

I'M READY, STEELE! LET'S SEE YA TRY!

ALRIGHT! COOL YER JETS, STEELE! YA *KNOW* THAT ENTO-MOLOGY IS DUKES'S SPECIALTY!

AH, SARGE! IT'S A CONCRETE BRIDGE, FER CRYIN' OUT LOUD!

NEXT: BATTLIN' BUGS!!

DIST. BY QUATERNARY FEATURES

"DON'T BE A FOOL, BILLY!"

JOHN CALLAHAN

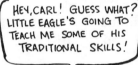

PETER SINCLAIR

ANY WAY YOU SLICE IT

A successful American executive flies to Tokyo on a business trip. As soon as he lands, he is warned by the embassy that he may be on a terrorist hit list, and that he should find himself a bodyguard. "Go to the Sony Building," he is told, "and on the fourteenth floor you'll find an excellent security service."

The executive hurries over, and is greeted by an elderly gentleman dressed in traditional robes. "You are most welcome here," he says. "I show you three bodyguards. You choose one."

The old man claps his hands and calls, "Number One!" In walks a big Samurai swordsman. The old man opens a jar and lets out a common housefly. Immediately, the swordsman slashes through the air with his weapon, neatly slicing the fly in half.

"That's very impressive," says the American. "This is my man."

"No, wait, please," replies the old man. "I show you Number Two."

When Number Two enters, the old man releases a second fly. Instantly, with two precise moves, the fly is cut into four tiny pieces.

"Incredible," says the visitor. "I'll take him."

"No—wait. You haven't seen Number Three."

Unlike the first two swordsmen, Number Three is short and scrawny. As the old man releases a third fly, "whoosh" goes the sword. But the fly is still moving.

"What's the big deal?" says the American. "The fly is still alive."

"Oh yes," says the old man. "Fly is still alive. But he never make love again."

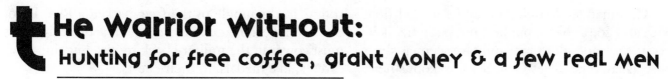

the warrior without:
hunting for free coffee, grant money & a few real men

BY IAN SHOALES

Once a week, I drop by the public radio station to see if anybody's left a grant for me. Fat chance. In today's economy, I not only don't get a grant, I don't even get a free cup of coffee. The Styrofoam cup by the break room coffee maker has "50¢" inked firmly in its side. Even if I did want to steal a cup of joe, every available mug has an employee's name carved into it. The fridge, well-stocked with lunches, swarms with snarling notes like, "This yogurt is mine!" or "Hands off!" It's pretty hostile territory, even for this bold freeloader.

On the upside, there's always a row of books on the counter, unsolicited reviewers' copies left for anybody who wants them. These stiff new hardbacks, post-literate America's abandoned puppies thrown heedlessly into the swift media stream, have washed up in the kitchenette's bright fluorescent lights, to be ignored by the underfed and overcaffeinated employees of public broadcasting. But not by this bold freeloader.

The books tend to be either thousand-page romances set in the Ice Age or aggressively dull nonfiction by obscure pundits, whose efforts are described in the jacket copy as "a wake-up call to America" by other obscure pundits. The last time I stopped by the free table, though, I really scored: *Rogue Warrior*, the ghostwritten autobiography of Richard Marcinko, the "Controversial, Death-Defying Founder of the U.S. Navy's Top Secret Counterterrorist Unit SEAL TEAM SIX."

I grew up on Richard Widmark frogman movies, so I read the book with the jaw-dropping admiration of a 12-year-old. I used to dream of growling to a grizzled unit, "Come on, you mud-sucking monkeys, into the drink, and let's make a stink. Doom on you, commie scum!" (I would've done it, too, if my draft number hadn't been 359.) Marcinko makes Gordon Liddy look like a desk jockey. He beats up Marines, slurps spaghetti through his nose, chugs Cambodia cobra venom and parachutes from a C-130 with 100 pounds of lethal hardware, all the while displaying an enormous capacity for profanity, drink and misogyny, and a command of military jargon that would have even Tom Clancy scratching his head.

Unfortunately, when Commander Marcinko was ordered to test the security of various naval bases, he imitated terrorist attacks with such zeal that enraged Pentagon pencil-necks drummed him out of the Navy and threw him some jail time to boot. That's his allegation. If his hands hadn't been tied by "chickens—t colonels" more concerned with chain of command than victory, this hardcase killer could have won any conflict you can think of, single-handed. Local public broadcasting ignores this message at its peril.

If this is the way the Navy treats its fiercest warriors, no wonder it seems to have worse morale than the Post Office. Top sailor brass certainly keep busy blaming underlings for everything from spontaneous ship sinkings and mysterious explosions to the now infamous Tailhook incident. Sure, some heads have rolled, but our tarnished armada's spin doctors wriggle on, most recently when the Marine Corps, angered over a San Francisco AIDS Foundation print ad showing a gay man with its globe-and-anchor emblem for a tattoo, threatened to sue. "You saying we're gay?" whined our few, yet proud, leathernecks. "You take that back!" I hate to admit it, but maybe Dan Quayle is right. If even the effing Marine Corps needs one, there probably are way too many lawyers.

Commander Marcinko may be a mad dog with an ego problem, but he's not pathetic. Is it just me, or doesn't today's military seem as slippery as lawyers? Does Gen. Schwarzkopf's new book, for example, kick butt and name names? That's a negative, gentle reader: All criticism is cautious. Today the private sector has all the savage raiders. But when neocon policy wonks and suspendered dudes in power ties threaten to break off your arms and beat you to death with them, why aren't they laughed out of the conference room? In the jungle of the free market, a Ross Perot can strut like a bantam brigadier; but actual brigadiers must cower in the military back rooms, hugging their careers, like medals, to their chests.

Maybe the lesson to remember is this: Swaggering males, both private and public, will do whatever it takes to get a book deal. There's a swelling army of ghost-writers traveling on its stomach, brave scribes shaping the image of modern men, both macho and silly, shaping the new American male's battle cry: "It's not my fault! Follow me!"

choose your weapon

GUN n. artillery, cannon, blaster, gauge (shotgun), gat, piece, iron, rod, snubby, snub nose, snub noser, snub-nosed automatic, lug, Saturday night special, six-gun, six-shooter, bean shooter, peashooter, popper, pop, equalizer, difference, speaker, mister speaker, persuader, convincer, hardware, heater, heat, Betsy, patsy, Bolivar, Oscar, roscoe, mahocka; Jerry, canister, canojerod, hog's leg, forty-five, deuce-deuce, trey-eight, smokepole, smoke wagon, zip gun, slim, belly gun, snug, spud, potato, stick, boom stick, tool, noise tool, toy, works, business, blow, bark, barker, bow wow, boom boom (WWII), biscuit, pickle, prod, copper-dropper, crowd-pleaser (police), scatter gun, bear insurance, chopper, chatterbox, Chicago piano, grease gun, burp gun (submachine), dumb gat, gagged gat, hush hush, sissy rod (silencer), sun gun, taser (electric shock), hang (balance).

Heavy Metal Tease:
phallic and metallic

Feel the fire of TEEZE—five heavy metal bad boys hell-bent on blowing out your speakers; wringing blood from your ears, and sending thousands screaming for more.

Seasoned veterans of the brutal one-night-stand club circuit, TEEZE has taken it one step further and produced its first tracks: "On the Run," "Hellraiser," "Looking for Action," "Leave Me To Burn," "Somewhere, Someday," "Midnight Madness," "Party Hardy," "Crank It Up," "When the Moon Is Full," "Going Away"…all of which were penned by the band.

Always a totally self-contained group, TEEZE travels on the road with its own tour bus, 30,000 watts of custom lighting, and a four-way 3,000-watt sound reinforcement system.

Luis Rivera is the dynamic front man of this outfit. One of the group's celebrated lady-killers, Rivera's high vocal range is often a piercing, if not painfully wonderful, experience. When Luis hunches over and grabs the mike till his knuckles turn white, it's only a matter of seconds until the P.A. is due for another vocal assault. When Luis roams the stage and growls at the ladies pressed in at the front, more than a few tears are shed—above and below the waistline.

Brian Stover is the newest member to enjoy the success of this group. Brian's uncanny feel for twisting tortured notes from his sax while flying through the air onstage has been welcomed with open arms by this crash-and-burn outfit.

Gregg Malack shares the lead guitar chores and also does an occasional vocal. Some uninitiated observers might think that Malack was permanently wired to a nearby 200 line—he's a constant blur of pumped adrenaline, frazzled hair, and slick leather.

Kevin Stover is the muscle and the engine room of this metal machine. Always rock steady and full of explosive thunder, Stover is a menace behind his sizable drum kit. At the end of any given night, Kevin might appear ready to keel over from the sweat and sheer physical strain. But he continues to hammer night after night—flailing arms and legs challenging his kit to withstand his nonstop abuse.

David Weakley, considered to be the perfect stereotype of the wasted rocker, indeed looks and (on good nights) lives the part. Weakley represents the darker side of this group; his sardonic, some say perverse, sense of humor has often lightened up tense moments between band and audience.

(by SMC Productions, the booking agent for TEEZE, a Philadelphia heavy metal band)

---

1. You are not a superman.
2. If it's stupid but works, it isn't stupid.
   —Murphy's Laws of Combat

What it be

What It Is	What It Be
Def	cool
dope	the best
fresh	rad
funky fresh	way rad
stupid fresh	the raddest
chill	kick back
ill	lame
perpetrate	pose
dis	talk shit
crib	pad
tip	johnson
jock	johnson
jammy	johnson
deep	intense
wak	tweaked
freaks	bettles
load	car
posse	homeboys
down	into your scene, babe
hard	tough
word	word

From "Word Definitions," a slang glossary in the June 1988 issue of *Thrasher*, the skateboarding monthly.

irony John the Mytho-poetic

Robert Bly Reads a Poem About Shame and K-Mart to a Group of Men

BY DAVID MCCLEERY

"Here is a little poem. But I will not play my balalaika because I don't really know how. I am a pathetic musician. In fact I do not even know how to tune the damn thing. But it is dramatic and that's what counts. Here then is a small poem about men, and about shame."

"Tonight in the snow I am walking through K-Mart.
I am looking for a man with a chest as wide as mine.
Here in the shoe department are the men,
banging on the big thick rubber boots with the steel toes.

I want to ask them to share their shoe size with me.
It will bring us closer to each other.
"Son," I say to one, "mine's a 10-double EE."
We share only a brief moment but I can tell he values my shoe size
and my experience as an older man.

Oh the joy of manhood!

And here are more men—
extending their fly rods in the sporting goods.
And here is a father alone,
eating a hoagie and drinking a coke the color of shame.
It is good I say to drink your shame
and wear your pants so that half your ass shows.

There is a fairy tale in that.
A fairy tale about the young man who wears his pants so low
that he can carry his billfold between the cheeks of his ass.
He pays out the ass for everything he buys.
But that is a story for another time.
Perhaps for the woods.

And there is my good friend Bill Moyers.
Bill is buying dish towels.
"Bill," I say to him, "a man washes but does not dry."
He turns away in his dark coat as if he does not know me,
and moves off shyly like a deer into the drapery department.
Bill Moyers never understood what it is to be in pain.

I take my small sorrow into the wilderness of the check-out line.
    The women look at me with fear.
I think I like that.

I find a cashier—a young male.
I set my package down carefully.
My face is the color of the box—pink.
The young man smiles. He does not understand.
"For a woman," I say, suddenly embarrassed.

"A little blood," I tell him.
"Maxi protection without the bulk.
Outstanding comfort and discretion."
I don't know what I am saying. It is pouring from me.
Perhaps it is that damn drumming in my ears.

"Superior coverage, added length," I tell him.
"It is the duty of men—
Ah… Ah…to go out and bring home the feminine products.
As my father had done, and before him—his father."

Finally I whisper into the young cashier's ear,
an ear as white and perfect as a nautilus,
"If I were a woman," I whisper,
"A real woman, a womanly woman, I'd bleed every day."

_____

"Isn't that beautiful? Can you feel the shame? Let me read that again:

Ah… Ah…to go out and bring home the feminine products.
As my father had done, and before him—his father.

Can you feel it?

My Initiation into Manhood ©1991 Stivers

One night when I was thirteen, men with spears dragged me from my room.

They took me to a theater where we watched Marx Brothers movies.

Then we looked at books of French Surrealist paintings and listened to Charlie Parker.

I never saw them again, but my life was changed forever.

A GATHERING OF BEARS.

Frankly, grow up and tell your inner child to get lost

BY FRANKLIN CRAWFORD

Forget about your complexes and start living. That seems to be the message in *Annihilating Your Inner Child: Who Needs the Little Snot?* a new book from self-proclaimed anti-therapist, Dr. Nilknarf A. Drofwarc (Backlash Publications, $25).

Drofwarc is the same iconoclastic scribbler who penned the bestselling paperback, *The Men Whose Lives Were Destroyed by Women Who Love Too Much.*

In *Annihilating Your Inner Child*, Drofwarc's premise is based on what he claims is the mistaken notion people have that they can't go home again.

"They couldn't be more wrong," he says. "The tragedy is that you *can* go home again. And again and again."

Drofwarc feels that many Americans are on a premeditated collision course with their own childhood and it's not healthy.

"Bad idea," he warns. "Better to just grow up and get on with your life."

According to Drofwarc , America has become a nation paralyzed by self-consciousness, a "horde of pathological navel-gazers sitting 'round in circles plucking their own pallid flesh and whining about their dysfunctional childhoods.'

"It's a lot of cosmic drivel, all this pre-lingual womb-sop about preciousness and the inner child. It's enough to make you open a phony business and fleece all the suckers who think it'll help them get on with their lives. Wipe the mother's milk off your chin and go to work, you lily-livered mal-contents. There's more to be learned in the mundane round of daily doings than from a stack of self-help books, subliminal tapes and shame-based charlatans.

"As a nation," Drofwarc continues, "we have turned every aspect of human relationship into a forum for abject scrutiny. And we worship this child—the child within, the child without, the abandoned child, the repressed child, the lost child—forget all these fantasy children. We're grown-ups; let's worship the adult within who's had to endure all this crap for the last however-many-years."

The idea of a pristine inner child buried under an avalanche of worldly demands who needs to be re-mollycoddled is the biggest hoax since the Trickle-Down Theory, Drofwarc says.

"Anybody who thinks about it for a minute will remember that childhood was a protracted and terrifying exposé on the inherent cruelty of Life. It was a time crowded with distractions designed to keep you from dwelling on the Ultimate Truth: Someday you would look just as old and move just as slow as grandpa and grandma, although you'd probably be dressed better when you died. Now there's a bunch of people who want you to go back there and reclaim your inner child. Leave him right where he is, somewhere between the Oedipus complex and long division."

Drofwarc says you can save yourself the $25 fee for his book by reciting three simple words: "Don't Look Back."

"Spare yourself my mangled prose if you can make that your mantra," he says. "Besides, anyone who buys a self-help book and succeeds with it, didn't need it in the first place."

ERNIE

by Bud Grace

CONTINUED...

END

PETER SINCLAIR

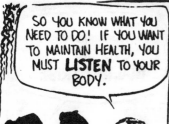

PETER SINCLAIR

Get in Touch with your Ancient Spear:
A Manly Seminar with Iron Joe Bob

BY JOE BOB BRIGGS

All right, guys, listen up.

It hasn't been our century, has it?

We kinda blew it, didn't we?

Even though you don't know exactly what I'm talking about, you kinda *know what I'm talking about*, don't you?

Haven't you had that morning where you wake up, look around and go, "Do I have to do this again?" And maybe you can't describe exactly what it is that's missing, but *something* is missing, right?

I'm here to tell you what's missing.

Your Ancient Spear is missing.

"Missing" is not quite the word. Maybe your Spear is broken, or maybe it's sagging in the middle, or maybe you just forgot how to use it. It doesn't matter. We'll get into the mythological aspects later, and you'll learn to Resurrect the Broken Spear, Mend the Sagging Ur-Spear, Launch the Warrior Spear and, of course, Spear the Psychic Fish. But right now it's enough to know that, well, let's put it this way: You're out of touch with your Spear.

Obviously I don't mean that you need to go out and buy a spear. If it was that easy, I'd be selling you a spear. Instead, I'm selling you a book.

No, what I'm talking about is something deeper, much deeper than a plain wooden spear or one of those spears with a lot of feathers hanging off it like Cochise had. Yes, what I'm talking about is richer than that, *richer even than Michael Ansara's spear*. I'm talking about the Golden Spear that lies at the bottom of the Soggy Gooey Lake.

Your true Spear is stuck in the mythic muck. All you have to do to get it back is start scooping the muck out of your psychic mind-swamp one bucket at a time. I'll never forget an experience I had one summer at a men's consciousness-raising sweat farm in western Nebraska. One Wednesday afternoon, a 38-year-old man from somewhere in the Midwest came up to me and he said: "Today I hated my father fully, and I remembered something he said to me once. He said, 'In or out! In or out! We can't air-condition the whole world!' And I realized for the first time how true that is. We *can't* air-condition the whole world, even though we try to do that every day of our adult male lives." We wept together for a moment. By the end of the summer, that man touched his Spear for the first time.

My point is that men don't know these things anymore. Men have lost touch with their Spears, their Maces, their Battering Rams, and what have they replaced them with? Weed Eaters.

We men fought an entire war in Europe so that a New Man could emerge in America, and what did we end up with?

Ward Cleaver.

Gimme a break.

Let's face it, it's been all downhill since then, hasn't it?

We're weenies.

We've *been* weenies.

Women have known this for a long time.

It took us longer to figure it out. It normally takes us at least 20 years in a relationship just to admit that, when we were kids, we liked to get the empty toilet paper roll and play it like a trumpet. So when you get to anything more serious than that, it takes a major life-changing cataclysmic experience, like six weeks in alcohol rehab, before we'll even *begin* to say anything like, "I am a weenie. I have never had a firm conviction, or even an opinion I cared about, in my entire life."

So lemme say it right here and get it over with:

WEENIES!

That's us.

Until you accept that, this advice will be of no use to you whatsoever. It's just like A.A. You've got to say that and *mean it* or we can't go on.

Here, I'll wait….

I realize I'm dealing with a lot of 34-year-old fat guys still living at home, watching too much "Star Trek" and leaving Doritos crumbs on their pillow. So I'll wait a little longer….

All right, have we all said it? Good.

Lesson No. 2: *YOU DON'T HAVE TO BE A WEENIE!*

I mean it. It's not too late.

Just because your dad spent his whole life building a toolshed, buying tools, putting the tools in the toolshed, repairing the toolshed, enlarging the toolshed—you know what I'm talking about, don't you? This thing that dads do where they keep buying tools but they never *do anything* with the tools—just because your dad did this doesn't mean you have to do it.

Think about it. How many times have you watched 37 college basketball games in a row on ESPN and then thought to yourself: "Who was that? Was it Villanova or Vanderbilt? George-town or George Washington?" You're disori-ented. You're confused. You're starting to feel out of control. So what do you do? *Go to a basketball game!*

How many times have you gone to the Ace Hardware store and bought $340 worth of stuff for the yard, including mulch, a tiller, a wheel-barrow-load of sod and one of those automatic poison-spraying devices that hook onto your gar-den nozzle—and then realized, when you got home, that you still had all the same stuff from *last year*, stacked up in your garage? You're reeling. You're wasted. You're losing the battle with modern civilization.

How many times have you read about bizarre sexual practices and said to yourself, "I wonder if people re-ally do that, or if they just make that stuff up to confuse people like me"?

All of these common ailments are part of being a weenie, but expressed in each one is the desire to *stop* being a weenie. But it's not enough just to finish the toolshed. It's not enough to start *using* the tools. It's not enough to remember the Vanderbilt score.

And, in fact, if you're reading all this and still think-ing, "Wait a minute, I'll ask my wife," then you're *not* getting it yet.

You can't just *decide* to stop being a weenie. The weenie lobe of the brain is buried deep in the cerebel-lum, where other people can't see it. And there's only one way to get rid of it.

Surgery.

Massive life-threatening surgery.

You've got to cut it out.

That's how I want you to think of this program. We're gonna be cutting out that weenie lobe and re-placing it with a new Mature Male nervous system. This is a shortened home-study version of my famous series of manliness seminars, which have been attended by thousands of weenies already. In fact, the first time I went on a Wild Man Weekend, it changed my life forever. You know what I'm talking about? One of those things where you go out in the woods with 20 other guys and put bandannas on your head and beat tom-toms together to prove you're not a wimp?

I'll never forget it. I sweated a lot. I cried. I sweated *while* I was crying. Of course, I was crying because they made me sweat so much. We had this one part of the weekend where we went in a giant sauna and turned it up to about, oh, 280, until everybody's skin turned the color of strawberry Jell-O and the veins in our fore-heads started exploding, and it turned into this com-munal out-of-body *male* thing, where everybody was screaming, "I want out of my body!"

Are you starting to sense what I'm talking about here? Put that Dorito down and listen. It's the Masculine Movement, where we get back in touch with our caveman selves. It's so *powerful*. You really can't understand it unless you've been there.

The Wild Man process involves five basic phases: Sweating, Yelling, Crying, Drum-Beating and Ripping Your Shirt Off Even if It's Expensive.

You may wonder why we do this stuff. It's because the modern American male has lost touch with his primitive self. They used to have a ceremony called Separating From the Mother. (Of course, they still do. It's called the "Get a job!" ceremony.) But now most guys *never* separate from their mothers. They think *all* women are their mothers, and so they expect all their girlfriends to take care of their emotional needs.

Once I understood this, I called up my mother to tell her I was separating from her.

"That's nice," she said. "I'm glad you have a hobby."

The other ceremony they used to have was called Initiation Into the Company of Men. Of course, we still have this one, too. It's called "beer." In primitive times they would ram crooked sticks through your breast, like in "A Man Called Horse," and then beat you with a Lincoln log or something until you felt like a man. But the modern American man never does this, and so he spends his whole life feeling *uncomfortable* around other men, and never talking to them about anything except football.

I hope you're following this.

That's why we start off with the lobster-sauna Sweating Ceremony. Then we move on to the Yelling Like Banshees Ceremony. Then we sit in a circle, and whoever has the stick gets to talk, and he's supposed to say stuff from *A Chorus Line*, like "I was always afraid I was a homosexual, and my father kicked my Tonka dump truck when I was 7 and I never got over it," until he starts bawling like a baby in front of everybody else.

Next comes Beating the Manly Tom-Tom. In order to get in touch with our real Wild Man self, we wail away on these drums and slam-dance against trees until we lose control and *become the drum*. Sometimes guys get so carried away they start screaming out personal stuff, from the deepest part of the primitive brain lobe, like "She divorced me because I never could stand her sister!"

And, finally, we get to the Ceremony of the Ripping Shirt, where we cavort around like apes in the jungle, exposing our manly flesh to the elements, revealing our manliness to other men, becoming true warrior-king-lover-gods that we always were, but Brenda Weatherby in 10th grade would never believe it. Then we make a conga line and dance out into the woods and plunge into the river and splash around until we feel manly enough to take off all our clothes and rip the guts out of a wild hog.

I felt so much better after doing this the first time. I went back to Grapevine, Texas, where I live, and I told my girlfriend, Wanda Bodine, everything I'd been through, and she said: "That sounds great. Did they teach you how to wear the same color socks on both feet?"

You ever feel like women don't *understand* just how manly we are?

It bugs me.

> It's the masculine movement, where we get back in touch with our cave man selves.

Anyhow, that's not the point. The point is that *you* could have all these same Wild Man experiences that I had. And I know what you're thinking, right at this very moment. You're thinking, "I ain't getting nekkid in the woods."

Don't worry about it. Really. That'll come later.

All I want you to know right now is that, if you'll trust me, if you'll clear your head, get rid of your old weenie preconceptions, give me a little slack, then you"ll feel a new male *power* rising inside you. You"ll feel the whole course of manly civilization rushing through your manly veins. You'll never feel like a wimp or a loser or a weakling again, for the rest of your life. We're gonna do this together. We're gonna be men. And *how* are we gonna do it? By doing the most manly thing that men can do together:

I'll tell you a fairy tale.

It'll be fun, really.

It's a good one.

It has a beautiful princess in it.

You're not buying this, are you?

"This is a twenty-four-year-old male, who was admitted last night with fever, chilling, and severe abdominal cramping. . . ."

HE FARTED IN THE SWEAT LODGE.

PETER SINCLAIR

White Men Can't Drum

BY SHERMAN ALEXIE

Last year on the local television news, I watched a short feature on a meeting of the Confused White Men chapter in Spokane, Wash. They were all wearing war bonnets and beating drums, more or less. A few of the drums looked as if they might have come from Kmart, and one or two men just beat their chests.

"It's not just the drum," the leader of the group said. "It's the idea of a drum."

I was amazed at the lack of rhythm and laughed, even though I knew I supported a stereotype. But it's true: White men can't drum. They fail to understand that a drum is more than a heartbeat. Sometimes it is the sound of thunder, and many times it just means some Indians want to dance.

As a Native American, I find it ironic that even the most ordinary moments of our lives take on ceremonial importance when adopted by the men's movement. Since Native American men have become role models for the men's movement, I find it vital to explain more fully some of our traditions to avoid any further misinterpretation by white men.

Peyote is not just an excuse to get high.

A Vision Quest cannot be completed in a convention room rented for that purpose.

Native Americans can be lousy fathers and sons, too.

A warrior does not necessarily have to scream to release the animal that is supposed to reside inside every man. A warrior does not necessarily have an animal inside him at all. If there happens to be an animal, it can be a parakeet or a mouse just as easily as it can be a bear or a wolf.

When a white man adopts an animal, he often chooses the largest animal possible. Whether this is because of possible phallic connotations or a kind of spiritual steroid abuse is debatable.

I imagine a friend of mine, John, who is white, telling me that his spirit animal is the Tyrannosaurus rex.

"But, John," I would reply gently, "those things are all dead."

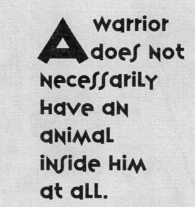

A warrior does not necessarily have an animal inside him at all.

As a "successful" Native American writer, I have been asked to lecture at various men's gatherings. The pay would have been good—just a little more reparation, I figured—but I turned down the offers because I couldn't have kept a straight face.

The various topics I have been asked to address include "Native Spirituality and Animal Sexuality," "Finding the Inner Child" and "Finding the Lost Father." I figure the next step would be a meeting on "Finding the Inner Hunter When Shopping at the Local Supermarket."

Much of the men's movement focuses on finding things that are lost. I fail to understand how Native American traditions can help in that search, especially considering how much we have lost ourselves.

The average life expectancy of a Native American male is about 50 years—middle age for a white male—and that highlights one of the most disturbing aspects of the entire men's movement. It blindly pursues Native solutions to European problems but completely neglects to provide European solutions to Native problems.

Despite the fact that the drum still holds spiritual significance, there is not one Indian man alive who has figured out how to cook or eat a drum.

As Adrian C. Louis, the Paiute poet, writes, "We all have to go back with pain in our fat hearts to the place we grew up to grow out of." In their efforts to find their inner child, lost father or car keys, white males need to go way back. In fact, they need to travel back to the moment when Christopher Columbus landed in America, fell to his knees on the sand and said, "But my mother never loved me."

That is where the real discovery begins.

Still, I have to love the idea of so many white men searching for answers from the same Native traditions that were considered heathen and savage for so long. Perhaps they are popular among white men precisely because they are heathen and savage.

After all, these are the same men who look as if they mean to kill each other over Little League games.

I imagine the possibilities for some good Indian humor and sadness mixed all together.

I imagine that Lester Falls Apart, a full-blood Spokane, made a small fortune when he gathered glass fragments from shattered reservation car-wreck windshields and sold them to the new-age store as healing crystals.

I imagine that six white men traveled to a powwow and proceeded to set up shop and drum for the Indian dancers, who were stunned and surprised by how much those white men sounded like clumsy opera singers.

I imagine that white men turn to an old Indian man for answers. I imagine Dustin Hoffman. I imagine Kevin Costner. I imagine Daniel Day-Lewis. I imagine Robert Bly.

Oh, these men who do all of the acting and none of the reacting.

My friend John and I were sitting in the sweat lodge. No. We were actually sitting in the sauna in the Y.M.C.A. when he turned to me.

"Sherman," he said, "considering the chemicals, the stuff we eat, the stuff that hangs in the air, I think the sweat lodge has come to be a purifying ceremony, you know? White men need that, to use an Indian thing to get rid of all the pollution in our bodies. Sort of a spiritual enema."

"That's a lot of bull," I replied savagely.

"What do you mean?"

"I mean that the sweat lodge is a church, not a free clinic or something."

The men's movement seems designed to appropriate and mutate so many aspects of Native traditions. I worry about the possibilities: men's movement chain stores specializing in portable sweat lodges; the "Indians 'R' Us" commodification of ritual and artifact; white men who continue to show up at powwows in full regalia and dance.

Don't get me wrong. Everyone at a powwow can dance. They all get their chance. Indians have round dances, corn dances, owl dances, intertribal dances, interracial dances, female dances and, yes, even male dances. We all have our places within those dances.

I mean, honestly, no one wants to waltz to a jitterbug song, right?

Perhaps these white men should learn to dance within their own circle before they so rudely jump into other circles. Perhaps white men need to learn more about patience before they can learn what it means to be a man, Indian or otherwise.

Believe me, Arthur Murray was not a Native American.

Last week my friend John called me up on the telephone. Late at night.

"Sherman," he said, "I'm afraid. I don't know what it means to be a man. Tell me your secrets. Tell me how to be a warrior."

"Well, John," I said, "a warrior did much more than fight, you know? Warriors fed their families and washed the dishes. Warriors went on Vision Quests and listened to their wives when they went on Vision Quests, too. Warriors picked up their dirty clothes and tried not to watch football games all weekend."

"Really?"

"Really," I said. "Now go back to sleep."

I hung up the phone and turned on the television because I knew it would be a long time before sleep came back to me. I flipped through the channels rapidly. There was "F Troop" on one channel, "Dances With Wolves," on another and they were selling authentic New Mexican Indian jewelry on the shopping channel.

What does it mean to be a man? What does it mean to be an Indian? What does it mean to be an Indian man? I press the mute button on the remote control so that everyone can hear the answer.

FOR YOUR NEXT MEN'S MEETING-
TRY THE NEW
TALKING STICK®
FROM
WRONCO!
YEAH, MY DAD WAS THE SAME WAY!
YEAH, NATIVE AMERICANS ARE, LIKE, SO SPIRITUAL!
HO!
GREETINGS BROTHER!, ARE YOU ON OUR MAILING LIST?
PULL THE LEATHER CORD FOR REAL "MAN TALK."
HI-IMPACT PVC PLASTIC
BATTERIES NOT INCLUDED.
PETER SINCLAIR

NATE SLOAN, ASTRAL AUTO RACER EXTRAORDARE,
GRASPING HIS PARADIGM SHIFT, SLAMMING ON
HIS PARTICLE ACCELERATOR, ON HIS WAY
TOWARD BEING EVERYWHERE, ALWAYS, NOW.

OFF THE DEEP END © 1992 Andrew Lehman

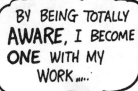

PETER SINCLAIR

THE WILD MAN WEEKEND IS DOWN THE HALL.
THIS IS THE STAR TREK CONVENTION.

Guy Stuff

Peter Sinclair

Frankly, patchouli oil can destroy your manhood

BY FRANKLIN CRAWFORD

A young man is standing next to me, reeking of patchouli oil.

OK, I don't like it, but it's one of the hazards of life here in Tiny Town, especially in some of the places I frequent.

However, on this particular occasion, he is really bothering me, this patchouli freak. Good Lord knows he's not harming anyone, so maybe I've got a Neptune-Uranus conjunction or some other bad transit because he's just standing there wearing dirty jeans and a tie-dyed shirt, hands in his pockets, looking stoned and exuding a fragrance that smells a lot like Spic n' Span, and I really want to slap him.

Cripes, I realize I'm getting to that point in my life where I'm starting to resent younger people. So what does a mature person do in such a situation?

That's right. A truly mature person becomes *patronizing and sarcastic.*

So here goes—an appeal to all young men who wear patchouli oil.

This is not easy for me to admit but, heh-heh, I wore patchouli oil once myself, boys. That was a long time ago and I was stoned a lot that summer too and my father thought I was "a hippy-queer" for wearing it, which only made me splash on more, not to be a hippy-queer, but to be cool.

At least I thought so.

Ah, callow youth. And to think I had a whole bottle of Jade East my mother gave me that I never used.

Understand the imperialistic roots, the politics, of your indulgence.

Things might've gone differently for my family.

Now that I'm older, I understand my father's point of view. He didn't hate patchouli oil just because he was a redneck butthead—he hated patchouli oil because it caused chaos in his sinuses, made him sneeze and put him a foul mood. In fact, as I get older, I come to see how patchouli oil caused a lot of the trouble in my life, and I only wish young men today would realize how patchouli oil is slowly killing their fathers.

Today whole seminars are devoted to repairing the damaged psyches of middle-aged men who've lost touch with their manhood and with their fathers. And much of the blame for this lies with cashmere shawls and patchouli. Yes. Once upon a time exporters of fine shawls from Kashmir packed patchouli leaves in their shipments because the fragrance discouraged moths. And, yea, back then a woman's shawl was not a shawl at all unless it reeked of patchouli and believe it or not, for a while this fragrance only wafted through the parlors of wealthy, arrogant, tea-sipping Brits.

Think of the disintegration of the royal family and consider how much of an effect this early patchouli business had on their current miseries. Understand the imperialistic roots, the politics, of your indulgence. You are not being cool at all. You are doing a very bad impersonation of a 19th-century mothball.

My father's words may have been harsh, judgmental and homophobic, but I understand what he was getting at. What his nostrils sensed went beyond the eccentricities of a rebellious adolescent. He perceived the pointless unravelling of a whole way of life, the end-times of MANHOOD as he understood it, of Old Spice and order and supper at six with the whole family. The smell to him was like an omen of the drifting, aimless days that lay ahead for his son if I didn't stop wearing that stuff. So he did what any good father would do: He told my mother to go in my room and throw it out while I was at school one day. And she did.

Boys, it happened late for me. Look at where I wound up. But there's still hope for you. Get rid of that crap and don't go back to it.

And maybe if you washed once in a while you wouldn't need it.

Yeh. And get a haircut.

PETER SINCLAIR

Overboard

by Chip Dunham

A.A. IN L.A.

CALLAHAN

"My name is Mort and I represent Chuck who's an alcoholic."

fortysomething: A primer
when nobody was looking, a generation turned a corner

BY JIM SHAHIN

I was toweling my feet after a shower, idly thinking about the rest of my life, when suddenly it hit me.

Socks!

Not just any socks. Good, expensive socks. Buttery soft. Rejuvenating. Like a massage. Socks not merely to wear as blister-preventer or odor-eater, but to cushion, nay transform, the life that was about to begin. For that life was the one that begins at forty.

I am not yet forty. But at thirty-nine, I can see it from here. Besides, in some ways, I might as well be forty. Not just because I am at its cusp and thus breathing the last warm breath of summer's youth, but also because I belong to that behemoth known as the Baby Boom generation. Where it goes, I go. And recently it turned a corner: When nobody was looking, the thirtysomethings turned fortysomething.

The signs are everywhere. Television, for instance: *thirty-something* is off, *Middle Ages* is on. Sports: Jimmy Connors, the eternal child, turned forty at last September's U.S. Open; he took it philosophically—"I guess it's hell being forty," he told reporters following his loss in the second round to (thirty-two-year-old) Ivan Lendl. And, the unkindest cut of all, music: Somehow, hearing Crosby, Stills, Nash, & Young sing "We can change the world" is just not the same when you're straightening your tie in the rearview mirror on your frenzied drive to the office through rush-hour traffic.

> **i am not yet forty. but at thirty-nine, i can see it from here.**

Enter: good, expensive socks. They're more than footwear. They're an attitude. They say: Hey, you made it. You've reached the point when little things make big enough differences to be worth the cost. Still, I felt the need to rationalize, and so I did. *Your feet ache all the time, right?* my inner voice said. *And your disposable income—spent not on records, concerts, and wild-hair travel but instead on plumbing repairs and children's clothes—hasn't exactly been the testament to envied self-indulgence you fantasized, true? So spend a few bucks on good, expensive socks. Sure, the purchase is frivolous and decadent. That's the point: You've still got it!*

Of course, no matter how good or expensive the socks, they are still just socks. And socks are not a source of inspiration. Comfort never is. So the very idea of them made me turn against socks altogether, and led me to another insight.

No socks!

That is, shoes without socks. I remember reading about some CEO who went sockless and how it was considered an example of his endearing eccentricity. Yes, that was the ticket. No socks! Not good, not expensive, not any. I'll keep my maverick soul and, in so doing, keep my youth.

Ultimately, this thought led me to the rueful conclusion that going sockless would not be seen as endearing eccentricity. Alas, I am not a CEO. Rather, I'd look like some poor schmo trying awkwardly and in vain to make a statement. About what, no one would be quite sure. But I would know. And the knowledge would haunt me: You are trying to pretend you aren't…*fortysomething.*

I grabbed for the straw called "thirty-nine." But it was only a straw; I knew down deep that forty was just a birthday away. I resigned myself to my fate. And with a sigh, I decided I may as well begin making the transition.

So I came up with a list to help me and other reluctant fortysomethings come to grips with reality. It's a partial list, and it is more cultural than chronological, (which is to say, if you meet at least three of the following criteria but haven't yet actually turned forty, well, as we fortysomethings say, what can I say?).

You know you're fortysomething if:

• the last concert you saw was Eric Clapton, Little Feat, Carlos Santana, Ron Wood, the Allman Brothers, or Bonnie Raitt;

• you currently use, or have used, any of the following words: groovy, far-out, right-on, or rap (as in "to converse" as opposed to a musical form);

• you've recently heard the name Kris Kross, thinking the Seventies crooner of "Sailing" fame is making a comeback, not realizing that Kris Kross is a young rap group;

• you listen to a classic-rock station and say things like, "Now, *that* was music!";

• you listen to a classic-rock station, period;

• you're not sure what Lollapalooza is and you haven't heard of raves;

• you haven't caught onto "Yo" as a salutation or onto "way" as an adjective, as in "way old";

• you own a collection of 45s.

That last one hurts me the most. It reminds me that my language is so heavily accented with generational references and slang that it sometimes seems I need an interpreter to anyone under thirty.

Take, for instance, the following three simple sentences:

I wanted to play a 45, but my turntable was broken. [Translation: 45s is shorthand for 45 rpm, revolutions per minute; in ancient times the term denoted small, flat discs made of black vinyl called "records." Forty-

fives is how America listened to music in its home between the century's two great pre-CD eras: 78 rpm records—big bands—and 33 rpm records—album rock. A turntable is the machine on which America played its 45s.]

I am bummed. [Translation: "Bummed" is a variant of "bummer," an exclamation of sadness or regret. If, say, you had been dissed, then you would be bummed.]

We just moved into a new pad and I wanted to listen to an old Beatles tune. [Translation: "Pad," was a common synonym for "home" or "house." The Beatles, as you've probably been told countless times, is the group Paul McCartney had before he had Wings.]

I have recently moved my family, and my turntable was indeed not working upon our arrival in our new home. (A fortysomething metaphor?) While packing, I came across records I had forgotten I owned—in fact, forgotten I had bought. Forgotten, truth be told, even had been made. Records by bands such as Cold Blood, Blue Cheer, and Humble Pie.

As if that wasn't bad enough, I found in my closet a shirt that was at least a couple of decades old and which can only be described as psychedelic. I remembered keeping it as a token from a bygone era, like one of those time capsules buried underground with directions to open fifty years hence. I didn't dare try it on. I'd be bummed beyond belief, even though I knew it'd be a rhetorical bummer. Because I didn't actually expect the shirt to fit anymore. *Face it*, I said to myself, gazing into that closet of memories: *You're not thirtysomething anymore, you're not twentysomething anymore, you're a couple of decades away from that shirt.* [Translation: Steely Dan song that. Oh, never mind.]

So, a few weeks later, on the morning that I had my socks epiphany, I decided upon a preemptive strike. I set about to demystify the age at which life is alleged to begin and started making another list (I think lists come with age; I don't remember making them as a youth). Having made a list recognizing reality, this list would help me deal with it.

First, I had to realize that I couldn't rely on the past. Things had changed since my parents were forty. (Have you noticed how nobody has card tables anymore?) Still, the fundamentals remain the same. The main one is that when you turn forty you cross a line. In your teens, you couldn't wait to be in your twenties. In your twenties, you feared the thirties might steal your youth, but because the whole Baby Boom generation was a study in arrested development, you shrugged arrogantly. But forty!

There's no getting around forty. At forty, we cheer age itself and those who represent its victors, like Nolan Ryan and George Foreman. It allows us to hold onto the possibility that we're not insignificant: We can still pitch the occasional shutout, we can still land a few good punches. We can still matter!

But if you are only as old as you feel, then we graying mantises of the Baby Boom generation may not know how to feel. Our collective voice has gone from Arlo Guthrie to, well, who? Donald Trump? Murphy Brown? Bill Clinton? Dan Quayle? Camille Paglia? That's why the guidelines: In blurry times such as these, I need all the clarity I can get. They're simple and there are only three of them—men, I don't seek complication the way I used to—and, thus, they by no means comprise a definitive list. But every life that is about to begin has to start somewhere. Mine begins here:

• If you must choose, buy a car more for the comfort of its seats than for the power of its acceleration. You go the speed limit these days, anyway.

• From here on out, don't physically help anybody move. A back is a terrible thing to throw out. Again.

• And don't, under any circumstances, even try to be cool. You'll just look silly. By all the known laws of groovosity [Translation: defness], fortysomethings, by definition, can no longer be cool. Staying current is the best you can expect.

Oh, and one more thing. Buy some good, expensive socks.

WHEN I WAS A KID — I USED TO DREAM OF WHAT I WANTED TO BE AS A GROWN UP. A TEST PILOT — A COWBOY — A BALL PLAYER.

NOW I'M FORTY. AND I'M NOT A TEST PILOT — I'M NOT A COWBOY — I'M NOT A BALL PLAYER — AND I'M NOT A GROWNUP. WHO EVER DREAMED IT WOULD BE THIS HARD?

JULES FEIFFER

Planning Your Male Midlife Crisis

BY DAVE BARRY

The past twenty years have seen tremendous advances in our understanding of these mysterious creatures called men—what motivates them; what kinds of complex and subtle emotions they're really experiencing underneath their brusque "macho" exteriors; and why they are all basically slime-sucking toads. Most of this understanding has been supplied by popular psychologists, dedicated men and women who—despite the very real risk that they will have to appear on the Oprah Winfrey Show—are constantly churning out insightful groundbreaking books with titles like:

• Men Who Hate Women

• Men Who Claim Not to Hate Women But Trust Me They Are Lying

• Men Who Okay, Maybe They Don't Hate *All* Women, But They Definitely Cannot Stand *You*

And so on. Reading between the lines, we can see that men do not have a terrific reputation for being dependable, lifelong partners in a relationship. In this chapter we will put on our pith helmets and begin to explore a major reason for this—namely, the midlife crisis. This is a phase that all men are required, by federal law, to go through, as part of the Official Popular-Psychology Schedule of *Male Lifestyle Phases*.

Male Lifestyle Phases

Age	Phase	Interests
0–2	Infancy	Pooping
3–9	Innocence	Guns
10–13	Awareness	Sex
14–20	Emancipation	Sex
21–29	Empowerment	Sex
30–39	Attainment	Sex
40–65	*Midlife Crisis Occurs Here*	
66–Death	Contemplation	Pooping

We can see from this scientific chart that if you're a male who has reached age 40, you should be preparing for this exciting lifestyle phase.

What Is A Male Midlife Crisis?

Basically, it's when a man, reaching his middle years, takes stock of his life and decides that *it isn't enough*—that although he has a loving wife, nice kids, a decent job, and many caring friends, he feels that he is trapped—that there is still *something more he must do*, something that we will call, for want of a better term, "making a fool of himself."

The first thing you have to understand is that this is perfectly natural. The midlife crisis occurs in virtually all males, including members of the animal kingdom. A good example is the caterpillar. He will spend a large part of his life on a predictable career path, engaging in traditional caterpillar activities such as crawling around and munching on the leaves of expensive ornamental shrubbery, and then one day, out of the blue, he'll say to his wife, "Dammit, Louise, I'm *sick* of shrubbery." She does not understand him, of course. Partly this is because she has a brain the size of an electron, but mostly it is because he seems like a complete stranger to her, a different insect altogether. Soon he has left her to live in his own cocoon, from which he eventually emerges with a whole new youthful "look"—wings, bright colors, gold jewelry, etc. As he soars into the sky, feeling fulfilled and exhilarated, free at last from the restrictive routines of his humdrum former life, Louise watches him from far below. She feels conflicting emotions: sorrow, for she knows that she has lost her mate forever; but also a strange kind of joy, for she also knows, as she watches his multihued wings flashing in the glorious golden-red glow of the sinking sun, that he is about to be eaten by a bat.

Fortunately, this rarely happens to human males. Unfortunately, what happens to human males is worse. There is virtually no end to the humiliating activities that a man will engage in while in the throes of a midlife crisis. He will destroy a successful practice as a certified public accountant to pursue a career in Roller Derby. He will start wearing enormous pleated pants and designer fragrances ("Ralph Lauren's Musque de Stud Hombre: For the Man Who Wants a Woman Who Wants a Man Who Smells Vaguely Like a Horse"). He will encase his pale, porky body in tank tops and a "pouch"-style swimsuit the size of a gum wrapper. He will buy a boat shaped like a marital aid. He will abandon his attractive and intelligent wife to live with a 19-year-old aerobics instructor who once spent an *entire summer* reading a single *Glamour* magazine article entitled "Ten Tips for Terrific Toenails."

And if this is a particularly severe case of the male midlife crisis, if this male has no idea whatsoever how pathetic he looks, if he has lost all touch with reality, he will run for President of the United States. This is why every fourth year, just before the caucuses, Iowa becomes positively infested with obscure, uninspiring, middle-aged political figures, racing around the state with an air of great urgency and self-importance, issuing "position papers," lunging out of shadows to shake the hands of startled Iowans, demonstrating their

concern for agriculture by frowning thoughtfully at pigs, etc. You see this on the evening news, and your reaction, as an informed voter, is "What is *possessing* these dorks?" I mean, it is not as though they are responding to some massive groundswell of popular support. It is not as though large crowds of voters showed up at their homes and shrieked, "Hey, Congress-person! Please go to Iowa and reveal the key elements of your four-point tax-incentive plan for revitalizing heavy industry!" No, these tragically misguided men are acting on their own, trying to deny their own humdrum mediocrity, seeking desperately to inject some drama into their lives, and we could view the whole thing as harmless entertainment were it not for the fact that one of them invariably winds up becoming the leader of the Free World.

I'm going to assume that you're not a member of Congress, and that you therefore have a certain minimum amount of dignity. Nevertheless, you will eventually experience a midlife crisis, and if you're not careful, it could destroy everything you've worked so hard to build over the years. This is why it is so important that you recognize the problems that arise during this critical phase, and develop a practical, thoughtful strategy for dealing with them. This chapter will not help at all.

What Triggers The Midlife Crisis

Generally the midlife crisis is triggered when a male realizes one day at about 2:30 P.M. that he has apparently, for some reason, devoted his entire life to doing something he hates. Let's say he's a lawyer. He did not just become a lawyer overnight. He worked *hard* to become a lawyer. He made enormous sacrifices, such as drinking domestic beer, so that he could afford to go to law school. He studied for thousands of hours, sweated out the law boards, groveled to get into a firm, licked a lot of shoes to make partner, and now, finally, he has made it. And then one afternoon, while writing yet another deadly dull formal letter to a client, a letter filled with standardized, prefabricated phrases such as "please be advised" and "with reference to the aforementioned subject matter," he rereads what he has just written, and it says, "Please be advised to stick the aforementioned subject matter into your personal orifice." He may not be a trained psychologist, but he recognizes latent hostility when he sees it. And so he starts to think. And the more he thinks, the more he realizes that he hates *everything about* being a lawyer. He hates his clients. He (needless to say) hates other lawyers. He hates the way every time he tells people what he does for a living, they react as though he had said "Nazi medical researcher." He hates his office. He hates Latin phrases. He hates his *briefcase*. He hates it all, just hates it hates it hates it, and finally he decides that he really wants to have a *completely different* job, something fun, something carefree, something like…hang-gliding instructor. Yes! That's it! He tried hang-gliding once, on vacation, and he loved it!

Meanwhile, somewhere out there is a middle-aged hang-gliding instructor who has just discovered that he hates *his* life. He hates not making enough money to own a nice car. He hates sudden downdrafts. He hate having to be nice to vacationing lawyers. What he really wants is a better-paying job that enables him to do something truly *useful* with his life. Yes, the more he thinks about it, the more he wishes that he had become…a doctor.

Of course, if he did a little research, he'd find that most doctors hate the medical profession. They hate getting sued. They hate the way everybody assumes that they're rich (they *are* rich, of course; they just hate the way everybody *assumes* it). They hate their beepers. They hate peering into other people's orifices. They wish they had a career with less responsibility and fewer restrictions, a *fun* career that permitted them to drink heavily on the job and squander entire afternoons seeing how loud they could burp. In other words, they wish they were: humor writers.

My point is that there's no reason for you to feel depressed about being trapped in Career Hell, because so is everybody else. Doesn't that make you feel better? No? Hey, look, at least *you* can put this book down and go watch TV if you feel like it. *I* have to sit here and finish this stupid chapter so I can meet my stupid deadline. You think it's easy, being a humor writer? You think it's *fun*, sitting here all day in my underwear, trying to think up new material? *You* try it sometime! You'd hate it! Especially the point where I'd give anything to have a job in which I could wear a nice suit and write in standardized, prefabricated phrases. As soon as I finish the aforementioned chapter, I'm applying to law school.

Is there any proven method for coping with a midlife career crisis? If you put that question to a group of leading psychologists, they wouldn't bother to answer you. They're *sick* of dealing with your pathetic little problems. They want to be test pilots. So I'll just tell you the answer: Yes, there *is* a proven method for coping with the male midlife crisis; a method that enables you to have the stability and security of a conventional lifestyle PLUS an element of adventure and excitement; a method that has been employed for years with great success by thoughtful, sophisticated male role models such as Batman. That's right: I'm talking about having a *secret identity*. No doubt you have often asked yourself, "Why *does* Batman have a secret identity? Why doesn't he just come out and announce that he is Bruce Wayne, wealthy millionaire, so that the police chief could simply call him up when there was trouble, instead of shining that idiot Bat Signal into the sky? I mean, what if Bruce Wayne doesn't happen to be *looking* when the Bat Signal is turned on? What if he's in the bathroom? Or doesn't he ever *go* to the bathroom? Is that why he's always sort of grimacing? Is that why he…"

All RIGHT. Shut UP. The point is that Bruce Wayne doesn't need a secret identity for any crime-fighting reason; he needs it because he's supposed to be a grown man, and his wealthy millionaire friends would laugh at him if they found out that he was wearing tights and driving around in a Batmobile chasing after the Joker (who, when he's not wearing *his* secret-identity disguise, is a gynecologist).

What A Woman Can Do When Her Husband Is Having His Midlife Crisis

If your husband is exhibiting signs of a midlife crisis, at first you should try to humor him. If he wants to buy a ludicrously impractical sports car, tell him you think it's a terrific idea. If he wants to wear "younger" clothes, help him pick them out. If he wants to start seeing other women, shoot him in the head.

WHY WOMEN OUTLIVE US.

MEN LOSE THEIR HAIR.

COMBOVERS

ME

THEN WE GIVE UP.

WOMEN WORK ON IT ALL THEIR LIVES.

MEN DON·T.

P.S. MUELLER

IT'S THAT SIMPLE.

O WHAT A LUXURY

BY GARRISON KEILLOR

O what a luxury it be
What pleasure O what perfect bliss
So ordinary and yet chic
To pee to piss to take a leak

To feel your bladder just go free
And open up the Mighty Miss
And all your cares float down the creek
To pee to piss to take a leak

For gentlemen of great physique
Who can hold water for one week
For ladies who one-quarter cup
Of tea can fill completely up
For folks in urinalysis
For little kids just learning this
For Viennese and Greek and Swiss
For everyone it's pretty great
To urinate

Women are quite circumspect
But men can piss with great effect
With terrible hydraulic force
Can make a stream or change its course
Can put out fires or cigarettes
And (sometimes) laying down our bets
Late at night outside the bars
We like to aim up at the stars.

O yes for men it's much more grand
Women sit or squat
We stand
And hold the fellow in our hand
And proudly watch the golden arc
Adjust the range and make our mark
On stones and posts for rival men
To smell and not come back again.

State of the Gender

BY CHARLES VARON

Fellow men, I am honored to have this opportunity to present to you the annual State of the Gender Address.

Ours is a gender which cuts across racial, class, and ethnic lines as few others do. Men are currently represented in over 187 countries; we speak over 700 languages; and in total population we are second only to women. *(Applause.)*

This year, men continued to take leadership in science, business, politics, and communications. Feature articles on members of our gender were published in leading newspapers, and men appeared on the cover of *Time* and *Newsweek*. *(Applause.)*

It's estimated that in the past year, men fixed 400,000 small appliances and nearly 36 million automobiles. Men hit an all-time high of over 14,000 home runs this year *(applause)* though male pitching also gave up over 14,000 home runs.

On the down side of the ledger, hair loss continued unabated in our gender, with an average adult male losing 0.31 square inches of scalp to personal deforestation. Genderwide, gentlemen, this amounts to a total hair loss of some 27 acres. *(Groans.)* This was offset only partially by the 43 million boys who made the transition from fuzz to facial hair.

In all, 193 million male rites of passage were successfully completed this year *(applause)*, the most frequently performed being puberty, marriage, and driver education. We can rejoice that testicular cancer is now 90 percent curable, and we have reduced to near zero the deaths resulting from athlete's foot. *(Sustained applause.)*

In Geneva, our negotiators worked tirelessly, as is their habit. But they are proceeding with caution. Years of mistrust and misunderstanding cannot be erased hastily. Clearly, some provisions of the proposed treaty are in the interest of both sides, such as cultural exchanges between men and women. But let us be clear: We shall not submit to anti-male guilt tactics, nor shall we agree to give up even one more rib. *(Sustained applause.)* Our negotiators will not betray the vision and pride with which our male ancestors founded this gender over 2 million years ago. *(Sustained applause.)* We may forget birthdays, we may forget anniversaries, but we shall never forget our founding fathers, those men who hunted and fished, who pounded out stone tools, and who gallantly forged the foundation of the gender whose engine we have kept running smooth lo these many years. *(Wild applause and scattered chest pounding.)* I ask you: Would those ancestors have allowed on-site inspection of men's hunting lodges and tree houses by women without reciprocal access of men to women's bookstores and coffeehouses? *(Shouts of "No!")* As we strive to find common ground with women, let us never forget that our two systems are fundamentally dissimilar. Their system is based on estrogen, ovaries, fallopian tubes. They give birth, we give advice.

Clearly, gentlemen, security is our most important issue. We have lived too long with the fear of war and violence. If this means we must eventually give up war and violence, then so be it. We will bite that bullet when we come to it. In the meantime, we must seek tougher punishment for playground bullies, strict monitoring of fraternity hazing, and the formation of a blue-ribbon commission to decide once and for all whether it's nature or culture that makes us so bloodthirsty. *(Applause, with scattered shouts of "Culture!")*

So let us move forward together. The unbroken chain of masculinity, of which we males alive today are but one link, cries out for us to take action. Let us remember that our sons today will be the fathers of tomorrow and the grandfathers of the boys of the 22nd century. And if we wait for our sons to solve these problems, we will be up past midnight and then it will be another day. (*Sage nodding.*)

Internationally, from Lusaka to Budapest, from Beijing to Naples, from Key Biscayne to Kiev, men are still men. When heavy objects need to be moved, we are there. Who builds the dams, who clears the forests, digs the graves? (*"We do!"*) I submit to you that it is we, the men. And wherever we are, whatever our garb—be it dhoti, kilt, pleated trouser, loincloth, or dashiki—we will continue to be men until the last drop of testosterone is gone! (*Wild applause and foot stomping; some dancing in the balcony.*)

Thank you very much, and good night.

"when is it we're supposed to get our rocks off?"

RICHARD STINE

WHEN THEY DRAGGED ME TO SCHOOL AT 5, I REMEMBER SCREAMING: BUT I'M NOT READY

WHEN THEY SENT ME TO CAMP AT 10, I REMEMBER SCREAMING: BUT I'M NOT READY!

WHEN THEY DRAFTED ME AT 19, I REMEMBER SCREAMING: BUT I'M NOT READY!

WHEN THEY MARRIED ME OFF AT 23, I REMEMBER SCREAMING: BUT I'M NOT READY!

WHEN THEY MADE ME A FATHER AT 24, 25, 26 AND 27 I REMEMBER SCREAMING: BUT I'M NOT READY — NOT READY NOT READY NOT READY!

FINALLY, AT 50, I RAN AWAY FROM MY WIFE, MY KIDS AND MY GRANDCHILDREN.

I'M NOT COMING OUT AGAIN TILL I'M READY.

DADDY! GRANPA! GEORGE!

JULES FEIFFER

"It's perfectly okay to cry. Just don't do it where people can see you."

i'm just a person trapped inside a man's body

BY P. S. MUELLER

A friend was recently complaining to me about a couple living next door to him. They had been fighting a lot, keeping my friend awake and driving his fiancee nuts. At one point the woman next door shrieked, "Be a man, dammit!" to which the fellow next door replied, whiningly, "How can I be a man if I don't know what one is?"

Evidently, my friend's neighbor hadn't been reading much of the alternative press. As if by some magically collective fit of insight, media everywhere have discovered that men are in pain, confused, confined by traditional roles, dying too fast, missing their dads, and miserable about never having become cowboys. What to do?

Enter: The Men men.

There are some who have blazed trails for those of us too timid or preoccupied to claim our rites of passage and discover the mythic warrior-self within. Poet-novelist-Man man Robert Bly is here to save the day.

A few years ago he began helping men recapture the benign yet powerful "wild man" through a series of meetings in the Minnesota woods. Bly and his enlistees would camp, bond, discover the fierce, nurturing daddy we supposedly deny we are, and then they'd all run through the trees and go "woof." All this would cost, but what's money where there's manhood involved?

Bly had the inside track for a while. He knew we were bugged by all this modernity and needed to free ourselves from the "bad daddiness" that has made this world an awful place. And now there are more groups, reports, seminars and counselors to the male psyche than you can shake a phallocentric stick at.

A word of warning, though: To take advantage of these new opportunities to enlighten yourself, you have to have a lot of free time and money....Or you can listen to me. I've got a few ideas.

A man is one of three mutually exclusive things: a monster, a mystic or a muddler. That's it, and I know it sounds overly simplistic, but bear with me.

A Monster

As a monster, you make war and oppress women. You subjugate, compete, acquire ruthlessly and hate yourself because you have no heart. You're the guy who drills the oil. You're the game-playing sociopath at the office who should be hunted down and shot. You leave big monster tracks all over the place, and you'll die without your daddy's approval, unless you change your ways and become…a mystic.

A Mystic

A mystic is a former monster who has seen the patriarchal error of his ways. As a mystic, you've learned what an evil thing testosterone can be, but are now channeling it positively. As a monster, you made a lot of money in the '80s, only to discover that in the '90s money is meaningless. And so today you spend it as a mystic, attempting to acquire the heart you never had to go with the head that got you in all that trouble in the first place. Mystics are better than monsters and muddlers. They've resolved everything. They are the warrior-kings with the inside dope on the grail market.

A Muddler

If you're a muddler you're kind of like Dagwood or Newhart. You're a nice enough guy. You try to get along with folks and probably put up with more than you should. You go to work for monsters, pay bills, and come home to read what the mystics say about your inadequacy. Though you're frequently confused by them, you actually *like* women. You don't have the venom of a monster or the insight of a mystic, but you do have the safe harbor of sandwiches and naps.

Muddlers also have a blind spot. Muddlers don't have the time, inclination, or money to spend on defining their maleness. In fact, they rarely give it a thought. Instead, muddlers are busy going about the business of being humans. Muddlers have friendships a monster doesn't need and a mystic can't believe we've earned. Yes, I admit it. I'm a muddler. I buy faucet washers, not slaves or salvation.

This formula applies to gays as well as straights. We all carry on within the various contexts of monsterhood, mysticality and muddlingness. A gay man might not feel at home in many of the male-awareness projects we'll soon be reading about in *Time* magazine, but gays fit right in here. I left out crazy guys too. And Masons. I may have left you out. But then again, I'm not trying to create an industry, just a newspaper article that will net me enough money for a few faucet washers.

I can't help thinking about that poor guy who lives next door to my friend. In the heat of the moment, most of us just sputter and grasp for inadequate words. Any old words will do. But I like to think that perhaps he paused, considered his sad remark, and then, lowering his voice so my friend couldn't hear, said, "You know I'm a man. Guess which kind."

CALLAHAN

"I'd like to talk to you about by abandonment issues."

Two therapists get ugly.

frankly, man was for the davenport made

BY FRANKLIN CRAWFORD

Man's best friend is his sofa.

Take away his dog, his car, his family, but don't mess with his couch. A man will kill to defend it.

The masculine image projected in mass media is too often limited to portrayals of men involved in some work or sport, perpetuating the myth of men as agents of industry, action-oriented, hunters. As if these pursuits were representative of what touched the soul of a real mensch!

In truth, nothing is more macho than a man at rest.

And when real men rest, they don't recline on Barcaloungers and Lay-Z-Boys: They hit the couch. Hit hard. And with much love.

For this reason I am devoting a whole column to exploring this fundamental, but misunderstood, relationship. But I am not going to waste time on the habits and customs of that lowly sluggard, the "couch potato," a slothful creature bearing little resemblance to the true "sofa-mensch." The former is a parasite; the latter, a noble being evolving along the passing lane toward "divan-awareness" or "sofa-hood."

Depending on his background, a man becomes acquainted with the couch at an early age, sometimes through the father, but quite often from the mother. At this stage, gender plays an unimportant role in determining how the male will meet "the divan within," and young girls are just as likely to lie about the couch as young boys.

Should a young man be couch-deprived throughout his childhood, he will unconsciously seek one out in puberty, perhaps at a girlfriend's house. There he will discover the deep satisfaction of "putting his feet up" in the daylight hours. He may even nap. The blissful sensations from his first diurnal sofa initiation leave a lasting impression upon the man, unless his parents have burdened him with "sofa guilt." Young men who suffer from severe sofa guilt eventually become pretend nappers—the kind of men who nap with "one eye open." As a result, they never experience the zen of couching and become unbalanced, shifty, maladjusted people. Watch out for them.

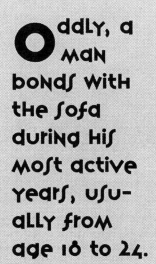

Oddly, a man bonds with the sofa during his most active years, usually from age 18 to 24.

Oddly, a man bonds with the sofa during his most active years, usually from age 18 to 24. This is a transient period, where the male "plays the field," and any davenport in a storm will do. It is not unlikely for men of this age to lie upon many different couches and experiment with a variety of postures.

Some may even attempt "the Dagwood Bumstead," napping with their faces toward the back of the couch. Any healthy man will tell you that this is an almost impossible napping pose, quite uncomfortable, and in some occult literature it's listed as a sign of either premature death or latent accounting skills.

There are, however, very good reasons not to "Bumstead," one being that it leaves the man vulnerable to a host of potential dangers, such as "the staring child" or "staring dog" syndrome, where a man wakes from a sweet nap, rolls over and finds his child or dog silently gazing at him for no reason at all. A man in the delicate, post-couch-nap state can get terribly frightened by this. No one knows why. But one man described it as "staring into the bottomless soul of innocence and knowing I had died." Most men who've experienced this never feel comfortable napping on the couch again in any position. Some go insane.

Another reason not to "Bumstead" is that it runs contrary to good couch sense. Working men who nap on couches imagine they are still a part of the waking world. They ride on the rims of consciousness. One of the great attractions of lying face-up, or face-out on the couch is that, at a moment's notice, the man is wide awake. Almost.

For example: A man watching football or The Frugal Gourmet starts "floating" (nods off). The wife or a child, seizing the moment, moves in and switches channels. Instantly the man's eyes open.

"Hey, I was watching that," he has every right to say—unlike a "Bumsteader," who has no defense.

"No, you weren't. You were asleep."

"Was like hell."

"You were snoring."

"Nonsense. I never snore when I nap," he says, betraying himself.

Note: Some men do not believe they snore when they nap and some deny they snore at all, ever. However, it has been proven that careless couchers will sometimes snore during sofa dreams, but wise couchers "swallow" their snores before anyone can hear them.

After a young man has slept with many sofas, he decides upon the most ideal and, either by luck or through an ad or by tireless search, finds the "couch of his dreams" and he may well be on his way to "foam heaven." It's a critical period, because the impatient man or one with low self-esteem often takes the first couch that comes along and this can prove injurious to the aspirant's development. You may observe men at this stage prostrating themselves upon absurd, ill-fitting settees, legs dangling over the armrests, their bodies in a running argument with the vehicle upon which they seek comfort. It's not unusual for men to abandon the couch-ideal altogether, preferring instead a bolstered straightback and ottoman combo, or, in extreme cases, *the chaise longue!*

Such men never mature.

Once the man has found his couch, it will be hard to part with it. He begins to explore "the divan within." He might even get an intuition, a glimpse into the hidden meaning beyond the mysterious phrase, "catching 40 winks." But usually, this does not occur until the man is well past 30 and has been employed in the private sector for a dozen years or more.

Women couchers are less common, perhaps because historically they "take to their beds," and by nature require a kind of privacy the sofa does not afford.

It is important that when a man chooses a woman, he learn her couching habits. If she is one of the few who desires true "sofa-hood," accommodations must be arranged so that both parties can pursue their couching without interruption. The invention of the L-shape couch was in fact the first step in this direction, and it's a shame more aren't available to the masses....A final note: For you who think that purchasing a convertible will solve this problem, save your money. That's not couching, that's cheating. And, besides, nothing should stand between you and your sofa when the inspiration is upon you. Yanking out a convertible is the antithesis to the high art of couching.

AT ABOUT FORTY
SOME OF YOUR
PARTS GO BAD.

MUELLER

PETER SINCLAIR

"I got a DWI, punched a cop and puked all over the judge's shoes. THAT should get me into a fraternity!"

Men's Group Visionary, 1953
I just thought, while we wait for our turns, we might just chat a bit about...
Oh shut up, Dave.
©1991 PETER HANNAN

Sid Fulcher, a graduate of one too many "Child Within" therapy sessions.

"Miss Jenner, please send in someone
who laughed at me in high school."

SUBCONSCIOUS COMICS

©1990 Tim Eagan

"May I be brutally honest for a moment?"

Wisdom of the Masters
on Masturbation

BY MARK TWAIN

All great writers upon health and morals, both ancient and modern, have struggled with this stately subject. This shows its dignity and importance. Some of these writers have taken one side, some the other.

Homer, in the second book of the *Iliad*, says with fine enthusiasm, "Give me masturbation or give me death!" Caesar, in the *Commentaries*, says, "To the lonely it is company. To the forsaken it is a friend. To the aged and impotent it is a benefactor. They that be penniless are yet rich in that they still have this majestic diversion." In another place this excellent observer has said, "There are times when I prefer it to sodomy."

Robinson Crusoe says, "I cannot describe what I owe to this gentle art." Queen Elizabeth said, "It is the bulwark of virginity." Cetewayo, the Zulu hero, remarked that "A jerk in the hand is worth two in the bush." The immortal Franklin has said, "Masturbation is the mother of invention." He also said, "Masturbation is the best policy."

Michelangelo and all of the other Old Masters—Old Masters, I will remark, is an abbreviation, a contraction—have used similar language. Michelangelo said to Pope Julius II, "Self-negation is noble. Self-culture is beneficent. Self-possession is manly. But to the truly great and inspiring soul they are poor and tame compared to self-abuse."

Mr. Brown, here, in one of his latest and most graceful poems refers to it in an elegant line which is destined to live to the end of time—"None know it but to live it, none name it but to praise."

Such are the utterances of the most illustrious of the masters of this renowned science and apologists for it. The name of those who decry it and oppose it is legion. They have made strong arguments and uttered bitter speeches against it. But there is no room to repeat them here in much detail.

Brigham Young, an expert of incontestable authority, said, "As compared with the other thing, it is the difference between the lightning bug and the lightning."

Solomon said, "There is nothing to recommend it but its cheapness."

Galen said, "It is shameful to degrade to such bestial use that grand limb, that formidable member, which we votaries of science dub the 'Major Maxillary'—when we dub it at all, which is seldom. It would be better to decapitate the Major than to use him so."

The great statistician, Smith, in his report to Parliament says, "In my opinion more children have been wasted in this way than in any other."

It cannot be denied that the high authority of this art entitles it to our respect. But at the same time I think that its harmfulness demands our condemnation. Mr. Darwin was grieved to feel obliged to give up his theory that the monkey was the connecting link between men and the lower animals. I think he was too hasty. The monkey is the only animal except man that practices this science. Hence he is our brother. There is a bond of sympathy and relationship between us. Give this ingenious animal an audience of the proper kind and he will straightaway put aside his other affairs and take a whet. And you will see by the contortions and his ecstatic expression that he takes an intelligent and human interest in his performance.

The signs of excessive indulgence in this destructive pastime are easily detectable. They are these. A disposition to eat, to drink, to smoke, to meet together convivially, to laugh, to joke and tell indelicate stories—

and mainly a yearning to paint pictures. The results of the habit are loss of memory, loss of virility, loss of cheerfulness, loss of hopefulness, loss of character, and loss of progeny. Of all the various kinds of sexual intercourse this has least to recommend it.

As an amusement it is too fleeting. As an occupation it is too wearing. As a public exhibition there is no money in it. It is unsuited to the drawing room. And in the most cultured of society it has long since been banished from the social board. It has, at last, in our day of progress and improvement, been degraded to brotherhood with flatulence. Among the best bred these two arts are now indulged only in private. Though by consent of the whole company, when only males are present, it is still permissible in good society to remove the embargo upon the fundamental sigh.

In concluding I say, "If you *must* gamble away your lives sexually, don't play a Lone Hand too much."

MEN

CONFUSED.

ANGRY.

SENSITIVE.

WORTHLESS.

COURAGEOUS.

VIOLENT.

PETTY.

MAGNANIMOUS.

WIMPY.

MUELLER

guy stuff • 87

PETER SINCLAIR

PETER SINCLAIR

CaN't Live With 'eM CaN't Live Without 'eM

"IT'S JUST THAT I'VE NEVER HEARD OF A 'SPERM DRIVE' BEFORE."

I KNOW WHAT GIRLS WANT

BY IAN SHOALES

At a party recently, a single woman friend expressed a healthy contempt for men in her social circle, whom she described as "…the Dysfunctional Boys' Club." How my heart swelled with pride. There I had been, thinking myself little more than a worthless sac of testosterone and cholesterol, but this simple phrase made me realize I was so much more—I was *dysfunctional*.

Do you know what this means? It means I had power over the lives of others, I could enable them in miserable lifestyles, turn a deaf ear to pleas for love and understanding, send them spiraling downward into the pit of despair. Once you hit pit bottom (as everybody knows who's ever read a ghost-written celebrity memoir), recovery is only a matter of taking the ladder of self-esteem up one rung at a time. I'm thrilled to be a man in the nineties, to be an invaluable part of woman's journey to inner peace.

Sure, there's a price to be paid—helpless sobbing at three o'clock in the morning, screaming matches over espresso in dim little cafes, and obligatory attendance at James Ivory movies are all part of it—but I believe it's worth it. When each relationship ends, as it must, with a woman hurling household utensils at your hunched back as you scurry through the door, you can scamper down the stairs knowing you've done your bit for intergender understanding. Indulge that self-pity, fellas! Drink yourself into a stupor with your worthless friends! You deserve it!

But before this healing process can begin, boys, you've got to have an actual destructive relationship. Face it, most males can't even get that far. Herewith, a few tips.

• Change your socks daily. One of the most frequent complaints women have of men is that they "smell like feet." The occasional bath and a trip to the laundromat can really lift a guy's sex appeal. In the early stages of a relationship, you might even consider having your socks dry-cleaned.

• Put the seat up before you urinate, and put it back down when you're done. Simple, but effective. In a related vein, arrange to have the object of your affection find you actually scrubbing a toilet. Believe me, her heart will swell at this sight. And if you get up after a meal and wash the dishes, she might demand sex right there on the kitchen table. After you've dried, of course.

• Say you like cats.

• Excuse yourself after belching.

• If you show up at her place for a romantic dinner, bring a nice '86 Cab instead of a twelve-pack of beer. You might also bring a Courvoisier bottle with you, for an after-dinner *liqueur*. It doesn't have to contain Courvoisier, though. Pour that into empty peanut butter jars, then fill the bottle with Safeway brandy. She'll never notice

> **I'm thrilled to be a man in the nineties, to be an invaluable part of woman's journey to inner peace.**

the difference. If she does, she certainly deserves better than the likes of you.

• Remember: *Thelma and Louise* was a milestone in American cinema, Woody Allen movies have now been revealed as the crude meanderings of a sick mind, and Madonna is problematic. It's okay to mock Robert Bly. Women regard men banging on drums in the woods with as much suspicion as you do. Skim Deborah Tannen, Susan Faludi, and Gloria Steinem. Don't venture an opinion about Camille Paglia until you hear what hers is, then agree with it. Don't take her to see *Reservoir Dogs*.

• Never get drunk unless she does.

• Never ask a woman why she's angry at you. She'll either get angrier at you for not knowing, or she'll tell you. Both ways, you lose. Ignore her anger. If it seems to go away, believe me, this will sow the seeds for successful dysfunction. If it doesn't go away, she'll soon be throwing crockery at your head. Either way, mission accomplished!

If you're a goal-oriented male—and what boy isn't?—fostering misery in yourself and others is Job One. Bad sex is just a perk. Keep that in mind, as you go home to nurse your bad boy's broken heart. Remember, you've got jars full of fine cognac back at the hovel. If that doesn't make you happy, nothing will.

"NEVER MIND YOUR ASTROLOGICAL SIGN—
WHAT'S YOUR NET WORTH?"

Wilt the Stilt

BY STEVE BHAERMAN

Wilt The Stilt, says his autobio
was one amazing lover guy-o
20,000 times he scored
postgame behind bedroom doors
20,000 passes, 20,000 dunks
(who says Warriors have to live like monks?)
In those days of sexual revolution
getting laid was no problem—
It was the solution
But scoring points by bedding maids
is risky in this age of AIDS
Is this evening's pet the one
who'll be a loaded roulette gun?
One bad call could get you kilt
Now *that's* enough to Wilt the Stilt

MARRIAGE PROPOSAL IN THE 90's

WILL YOU BE MY CODEPENDANT?

OFF THE DEEP END

©1990 Andrew Lehman

Men have that "Why" chromosome.

"Women are unpredictable, untrustworthy and I'm through with them forever. By the way...are you single?"

everything you always wanted to know about sex

BY JOHN BONI, M.D.

How big should a normal penis be?

Someone once asked Confucius how long his feet should be, and the wise old philosopher answered, "Long enough to keep you from bumping into things." A normal penis should be big enough to do the job of depositing Mr. Sperm into the watchamacallit so that it meets Miss Egg and makes a baby.

But how big is that?

Obviously, everyone's must be big enough because a tiny-penised race couldn't have survived. On the average, though, the normal adult-male penis is six and one quarter inches from base to tip in its tumescent state. When erect it should measure approximately twelve inches, but slight variations bring this figure down to eleven inches and up as high as thirteen—certainly not unlucky for *that* organ's owner. The diameter of the penis rarely varies much either way from the standard two and a half inches.

You said something about size not being important?

Exactly the point I want to make. It's performance that counts. Even men with only nine inches to their credit manage an adequate sex life with an understanding partner and some easily available artificial aids.

What is an erection?

An erection is nothing more than a reflex action, like the knee-jerk response, but don't go around hitting your penis with a little rubber hammer every time you want one. Some slight penile stimulation, like rubbing or stroking, is enough to bring a soggy organ to life. The brain has nothing to do with it. Publishers of nudie magazines know this but publish tons of these "erotic" periodicals anyway. This is for the benefit of the poor, lonely unfortunates who have no one to rub their penises, and so they rub them with the magazines instead. It gives them an erection all right, but no magazine ever said, "I love you, Joe." You can't get an erection just by *looking at something*. If you do, get a checkup. You may have cancer.

How does an erection actually happen?

You shouldn't ask this question. Erection is such a delicate, complicated process that it makes a rocket launching look like child's play. It's a minor miracle that it happens at all, and each erection you get may well be your last. It all hinges on the general well-being of the body—a head cold, hangnail, indigestion, money worries, anything, and you can kiss your erection good-bye. As far as the actual mechanics, the less said the better. If you knew all that's involved and all that can go wrong, you'd never have an erection again.

What happens to the erection after intercourse?

Nothing. It should still be there, ready and waiting. Intercourse actually maintains the erection. The penis, after all, is a muscle, and muscles stay firm with exercise. Intercourse is the penis's exercise and maintains the erection long after intercourse or, more exactly, ejaculation, is completed. The biggest complaint I get is from men who sex it up during lunch hour: "How can I get my erection to come down after I've finished intercourse? I can't show up at the board meeting like this." Of course, this problem doesn't affect people who suffer from that sexual nightmare "neuresy."

Neuresy? What's that?

An unusual condition in which a man loses his erection once intercourse has been completed.

What causes neuresy?

Frankly, no one knows, though cancer may be the culprit. Surgery can sometimes provide temporary relief in stubborn cases, but neuresy, like impotence, is usually irreversible. You can't teach a dead dog new tricks.

What about impotence?

Impotence is a very rare condition in which a man is unable to obtain any kind of erection at all. Real impotence is like natural blond hair—there's a lot less of it than meets the eye. Ninety-nine times out of one hundred, there's some other explanation: sloppy Swedish doctors, too much "extracurricular activity," unconscious dislike of the sex partner, latent homosexuality, excessive self-abuse, cancer, etc. I haven't run across a genuine case in over thirty years of practice, so forget about it.

I'd still like to know a bit more about it.

Well, so far as I know, there are only two kinds, but don't quote me—I'm not up on it (no pun intended). As I said, it is a very rare disorder, and most of the information I've been able to find on it comes from colleagues working in mental institutions, slum areas, and underdeveloped countries. The first kind is total impotence. Here, nothing works to produce an erection. All the ordinary stimuli—naked girls, magazines, paper bags, string, yogurt, etc.—have no effect on the bashful organ. A frustrating variation on this is the case in which a man carries his erection everywhere he goes—on buses, trains, walking down the street—but when he approaches a girl with an exposed whatzis, it drops dead on him.

What is premature ejaculation?

There's a lot of confusion and misunderstanding over this condition because it is so difficult to distinguish from one of the main symptoms of degenerative paresis. It occurs when the man inserts his erect penis into the thingamabob and begins his first thrusting motion. Before you can say "Draw!" the man ejaculates. His anxious penis is so quick on the trigger that it fires prematurely and has nothing left for the showdown at the O.K. Corral.

How common is this condition?

It's practically unknown. Nature usually equips men with enough built-in controls to hold ejaculation at bay for as long as they want—five, ten, twenty, even forty minutes—in order to save it for a properly romantic moment, when his partner says it's okay, or when the phone rings.

How often should a man be able to have intercourse?

That depends upon how old he is. If you're talking about a normal man of average age, I'd have to say a minimum of five or six times a day.

What about a man in his fifties or sixties?

That's the age I'm talking about, and the intercourse rate is five or six times a day. This rate drops significantly to about twice a day when a man reaches seventy, but, frankly, a man's sexual powers disappear only when he's dead.

Are there any sexual problems for men in their forties?

Only one as far as I can see: a sexually exhausted wife.

Some men in their prime claim they can ejaculate about ten or twelve times a night. Is this a put-on?

Hardly. They're either being very modest or openly admitting a problem in this area. As most people know, fifteen or twenty times a night is about average.

A good rule of thumb is approximately two ejaculations per penis inch (erect).

Is masturbating wrong or harmful?

I'm reminded of the old story about the parent who caught his son masturbating in the bathroom:

Father (ominously): You keep doing that and you'll go blind.

Son: Then I'll do it just until I need glasses.

This humorous anecdote is indicative of the misinformation about the Solitary Sport. Masturbating isn't wrong. It will do nothing to your eyes, your ears, nose, or throat; nor will it cause hair to grow on the palms. If anything, and the evidence on this is by no means conclusive, masturbation may, in some cases, inflict a mild insanity upon the habitual penis-pumpers. Besides this negligible drawback, masturbation weakens the penis somewhat. Each masturbatory act is equivalent of ten bouts of intercourse. Since each man is allowed only about ten thousand ejaculations per lifetime, it would be well to teach the young, apprentice masturbator to begin counting, or at least to start parceling them out to best advantage. Personally, I reject the ten-thousand figure as much too low. The amount is probably closer to twenty thousand, using the two-thousand-per-penile inch (erect) guideline. Women, on the other hand, can have as many orgasms as they can handle.

How can you tell if a woman has had an orgasm?

For openers, don't ask the woman, because she'll lie to you every time. Instead, look for the slight rash that shows up on a woman's feet immediately after orgasm. If you're performing in the dark, though, you won't be able to spot this telltale skin-change. For my money, the surest way is aural. All women say things like "Oh! Oh! Oh!" or "Oh my God!" as they experience orgasm. Some go "Brrrr," as if shivering from the pleasant sensation. If your partner doesn't moan and/or groan like this, then she hasn't experienced orgasm and is probably a Lesbian or just saving it up for that lifeguard. In one case I know of, the girl was dead.

How many kinds of orgasm are there?

Two: vaginal and clitoral. There has been a great deal of nonsense written in recent years about vaginal orgasm being a myth, but it's all hogwash. A woman should either have vaginal orgasm or a hysterectomy; if she can't have the first, she'd better have the second in a hurry.

What about cunnilingus and fellatio?

With today's liberal attitudes toward sex, many people freely engage in practices that were once considered immoral, sinful, and unnatural. I see no reason why these practices shouldn't be part of every person's sexual repertoire, provided they can adequately bear up under the unavoidable guilt feelings such perversions cause. Then, too, there is the aesthetic factor to be considered. If the man can withstand the unpleasant, fishy, and acrid odor during cunnilingus, fine. As for fellatio, there is some evidence, still incomplete and fragmentary, of a link between oral sex and lip cancer. And as an odd footnote to the fluoride controversy of the fifties, a Finnish doctor has discovered that concentrations of fluoride five times higher than the amount required to cause cancer in the gonads of laboratory mice regularly occur in the human mouth for roughly an hour after brushing with most commercial toothpastes. A word to the wise!

Is there such a thing as an aphrodisiac?

Yes, and I suppose that uppermost in everyone's mind is Spanish fly, the schoolboy's legendary dream chemical. There are others, like cow urine, common thermometer mercury, and pond scum, but none is as powerful as Spanish fly. In humans, one-tenth of one gram is enough to "turn on" the most frigid female; a larger amount spells sexual catastrophe, as evidenced by the insatiable lust of a certain young lady who was fed one gram of the stuff and impaled herself to death attempting intercourse with the gearshift of a 1961 Volkswagen. Of course, everybody's heard that old chestnut of a story a thousand times from a thousand different sources, but I knew the girl personally.

Are some foods *sexier* than others?

Eat an oyster and watch a limp organ bounce to life....Create the penis of your dreams with an olive sandwich....Unfortunately, this isn't the case. Food like sausages, celery, carrots, i.e., foods "shaped" like the penis—especially bananas and raw snake—are the ones that will increase penile length and endurance. It's as simple as that. Oysters, shrimp, olives—all that is a lot of bunk. A simple guideline is "Like breeds like," unless you find an oyster shaped like a penis.

Is it possible to tell penis size without seeing it?

A fascinating sidelight of a recent head-cold symposium was the discovery that the length of a man's nose corresponded to the length of his penis. A long or prominent nose indicated a below-average penis, while a small- or "button"-nosed individual usually had a penis above the average. Just remember: big nose, little hose; big hose, little nose. Actually, a more exact method is to measure the distance of a man's open, outstretched hand from thumb tip across the palm to pinkie tip and multiply by two; also, four times the length of a man's tongue will give you his exact penis length (erect). (Be sure the tongue is also erect when you measure it.)

As for men who'd like an idea of the size of a woman's doohickey, look to the lips. A big mouth means a big you-know-what.

What effect does childbirth have on sex?

Children do have a habit of hanging around every time their parents are in the mood. Outside of that, however, the damage of childbirth has been completed. A baby is much larger than a penis, and at birth it stretches the woman's gismo on the way out. The husband's poor penis flounders around inside like a BB in a boxcar, and neither partner feels a thing. Sex then becomes pointless. Nature, however, again compensates by decreeing that childbirth permanently ruins the figure and speeds up the aging process, making the mother less desirable.

Does VD only affect sexual organs?

No, some sexual adventurers have been known to contract syphilis of the lips, tongue, and even tonsils. Fetishists report a high incidence of syphilis of the toes. VD in these areas is rarely as serious but can be embarrassing. For example, unless you're an artist, you're going to have a hard time explaining a missing ear.

Are there other kinds of VD besides these two?

You bet. One in particular is called chancroid, an innocuous name in view of the damage it does. In the early stages, the chancroid penis becomes riddled with holes. Urination is accomplished in a spraylike drizzle. This might be fine for watering a plant, but it's terrible on the wardrobe. In the second stage the testicles begin to shrink. Sores form on the penis, which fills up with dead cells and pustules. If any of this pus comes in contact with your body or someone else's, it's skin-rot time. In the final stages the sufferer can get a job as a pile of oily rags or a compost heap.

Is it better to have sex with a virgin?

Most experts generally agree that it's better, and healthier, but also a lot noisier. Virgins tend to scream and yell and cry during their first intercourse. Just say things like "I love you" or "We'll get married as soon as Dad says I'm old enough," and she'll calm down considerably. About the only drawback is the high death-rate of virgins during their first intercourse—about 4 percent in the U.S., far higher than the rates in Scandinavian countries.

Is circumcision desirable?

Yes and no. Circumcision usually results in a severe loss of penile length. However, failure to circumcise a penis can result in cancer, in which case the penis must be removed surgically. The choice is in your hands.

Who enjoys intercourse more—men or women?

That's like asking which came first, the chicken or the egg. It's a question that just can't be answered, and, frankly, it's most often asked by men with feelings of sexual inferiority or doubts about their virility. After all, men and women derive sexual pleasure from different sources, and how can you compare what a woman feels when her earlobes are whipped with, say, what a man feels when his nostrils are filled with room-temperature cheese dip? Should the characteristic "orgasm flashback" that most normal men experience ten to twenty minutes after orgasm be included? Does a woman's periodic "vomit of Venus" count?

As you can see, the whole thing is silly. It all depends on the individual. A more sensible question for a man to ask would be, Is she enjoying it too much? If your female partner seems to be enjoying it a lot more than you are, there's something wrong—with her, not you—and you should consult your doctor. Of course, since all healthy couples achieve orgasm simultaneously, it may be a little hard to tell who's enjoying what, but concentrate—it's very important. Just as the praying mantis kills her mate during intercourse to heighten her pleasure, the overly responsive female can kill you.

"Ok, so all you think about is sex. So what's the problem?"

"Erection is chiefly caused by scuraum, eringoes, cresses, crymon, parsnips, artichokes, turnips, asparagus, candied ginger, acorns bruised to powder and drunk in muscadel, scallion, sea shell fish, etc."

—*Aristotle*
(Greek philosopher), *The Masterpiece*, 4th century B.C.

"Sex without class consciousness cannot give satisfaction, even if it is repeated until infinity."

—*Aldo Brandirali*
Secretary of the Italian Marxist-Leninist Party, in a manual of the party's official sex guidelines, 1973

"[Semen] descends principally from the liver."

—*Vincent of Beauvais*
(French philosopher and scientist), *Speculum naturale*, 1244–1254 A.D.

"A great portion [of semen] cometh from the brain."

—*Ambroise Paré*
(French physician and surgeon), *De hominis generatione*, 1573

"[I saw] in the human sperm, two naked thighs, the legs, the breast, both arms, etc....the skin being pulled up somewhat higher over the head like a cap."

—*Stephen Hamm*
Dutch naturalist, reporting what he saw through his microscope, 17th century A.D.

hicker son /stanfill

"I know I'm not Mr. Right . . . but how about
Mr. Right Now?"

Swami Speaks Out About Safe Sects
A penetrating interview

WITH SWAMI BEYONDANANDA

(Are enlightened beings meant to have sects? Or can sects actually stunt our spiritual growth, not to mention endanger our health? With the recent concert about Oughtism—a highly contagious swelling of the onus known to be transmitted through sects—many metaphysicians wonder whether the safest sects would be no sects at all. In this penetrating interview, The Yogi From Muskogee tells us everything we always wanted to know about sects.)

Us: Swami, let's get right down to it. What is your position on sects?

Swami: You see? That is just the problem. Everyone is so hung up on positions! People always want their sects to be on top and the other sects on the bottom. So I suggest we forget about positions. Let's go for sects equality.

Us: Well, what I mean is, how do you feel about sects?

Swami: You know, some people say we are all one anyway, so why do we need sects? Why make sects distinctions? It is true, that when you look beyond sects we are the same, but the differences are what make life interesting. Could you imagine a world without sects? It would be boring indeed. So I'm totally in favor of sects. In fact, I try to have sects in every town I visit.

Us: Some spiritual leaders would disagree with you. For example, Rev. Tim Tayshin of the "Mortal Majority" says he finds sects disgusting.

Swami: Oh, without a doubt sects can appear disgusting, as anyone who's ever watched two dogmas go at it can testify. And I agree that sects without love can never bring real pleasure. But

sects need not mean struggle and conflict. Sects can be really beautiful when people appreciate their differences. So let's not get sects mixed up with *sectsism*. It is not right when people believe their sects to be superior. We need better sects education to teach people to love and respect members of the opposite sects.

Us: One of the concerns about sects is that powerful gurus or organizations will force people into sects against their will. What do you think about that issue?

Swami: Oh, no. This is very bad. Sects must always be consensual.

Us: Well, then, what shall we tell our children? Do you believe there can be "safe sects"?

Swami: I think we worry too much about our children because of our own fearful and negative experiences with sects. Sure, there have been a few sects crimes—and Oughtism is one of the most virulent diseases on the planet, and we all know it is transmitted through sects. But why should that give sects a bad name? Let's face it, as soon as kids are old enough to walk around the corner, they are going to learn about sects anyway. So by all means, we should alert them about the dangers of unsafe sects. I tell young people that sects between consenting adults is fine as long as you're not obsessed with it. And it's pretty easy to tell when someone is obsessed. You see these people proselytizing door-to-door or selling flowers on the street or throwing waste products on those whose sects preference is different from their own—one look in their eyes will tell you they'll do anything for sects . And let's face it, unbridled sects can lead to unwanted misconceptions, and goodness knows we already have enough of these in the world. That's why I suggest that if you're going to engage in sects, you wear a protective sheath of white light. And no matter how ecstatic you get, keep your eyes open, okay?

Us: Do you think people should be able to change their sects?

Swami: Certainly! I myself started as a Methodist (actually my father was a Methodist and my mother was a Catholic, so technically I'm a Rhythm Methodist), but very early began to experiment with all kinds of sects. In high school they called me a sects deviate because I used to dress in the clothing of the opposite sects—you know, I would wear turbans and dhotis and saffron robes. Finally, I realized I would never find the kind of sects that turned me on in Oklahoma, so I moved to New York to put my sects change into operation.

Us: What about recreational sects?

Swami: Well, it stands to reason that in a society where recreation is so important, you're going to have recreational sects. I mean, think how many golfers look at their Sunday at the country club as a religious experience. Of course, recreational sects can also be pretty bizarre like those people who get their jollies buying and selling players in fantasy baseball leagues. And certain kinds of kinky recreational sects can be harmful too, like those people whose primary fulfillment comes from calling 900 numbers.

Us: So telephone sects is dangerous?

Swami: Sure. A lot of people who engage in this practice end up with hearing AIDS.

Us: One last question. Is there any general advice you'd like to give our readers about sects?

Swami: Yes. Remember, it is a natural thing for humans to have sects . So there is no need to feel guilty. And don't worry about the Second Coming. Don't worry about anybody coming. Just enjoy the moment right now, and be sure to love everybody regardless of sects.

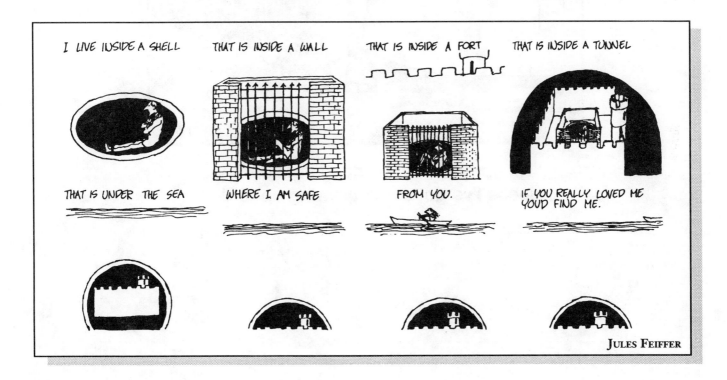

"I'm sorry it's not working out, Marsha. I
guess I've got some growing up to do."

Increasing abnormality in the sexual behavior pattern of the male black widow spider

By W. Henri Kriecker, D.E.*

Over the years I have enjoyed studying entomology, as a hobby. The study of insects is indeed a fascinating subject. There are almost countless genera. One could spend a lifetime studying butterflies, for example, and still not know all that there is to know about this group of insects.

More recently I have begun the study of the arachnids or spiders, which are—strictly speaking—not insects, and in particular, black widow spiders (*Latrodectus mactans*).

I have made some remarkable observations. I say remarkable because in checking through the works of Fabre, Gertsch, Emerton, Bristowe and Comstock, I found no reference to the phenomena I have observed, which had to do with the male of the black widow spider family. The male is considerably smaller than the female.

It is generally known that the female black widow, which is venomous, usually destroys the male immediately after mating. Frequently she devours the male after killing it. I have observed this practice on several occasions. Authorities on spiders have given no satisfactory explanation of this androcidal tendency, nor have I one.

Carried away with ecstasy—or utter contempt—the female destroys the male after mating.

Devouring Passion

The disposing of the male takes place immediately after mating while the male is completely spent from the orgasm. There is no respectable waiting for the ardor to cool. One authority has suggested that the female black widow is invariably disappointed in love, since the male is so much smaller, and exhibits her utter contempt by promptly destroying the male.

Another researcher speculates that the female black widow may be completely carried away with ecstasy and with unbridled emotion destroys the male.

Among human beings the saying, "I love you so much I could eat you," is not uncommon. The annals are replete with cases of teenagers' so-called necking wherein what practically amounts to mayhem was perpetrated, frequently stitches having to be taken.

Kucharov has suggested that the female black widow may be completely unstable emotionally and as a result is filled with mistrust. Fearing the peregrinations of the male during her gestation period she may put her mind at ease by destroying

*Distinguished Exterminator

him, then cozily hatching her brood.

A French authority has suggested that the female black widow may be likened to Shah Jehan of Agra, India, who commissioned the Taj Mahal to be built and upon its completion destroyed the builder so that he could never construct anything more beautiful than the Taj Mahal. However, this explanation hardly seems plausible.

It is quite obvious that the libido of the male black widow is strong or else it would not yield to the mating instinct with almost certain death staring it in the face. This would be uxoriousness beyond the call of duty. On the other hand, the male may have been conditioned, down through the ages, to believe that death is not too dear a price to pay for the utter gratification of mating. One would have to mate with a black widow spider to know for certain whether it was worth paying for with one's life. It would appear exorbitant. The Italians, however, have a saying, "See Florence and die" (referring to the city, of course).

Gay Life, Spider Style: oh what tangled webs they weave when first they practice to conceive.

Out of the Closet
By careful scrutiny of the minute creatures I have learned that there is a growing tendency upon the part of the male black widow to weigh the pros and cons of mating. Some of the young bucks have adopted a "fools rush in where angels fear to tread" attitude. As a result, there is a lessening of the black widow spider population. This is favorable since they are dangerous to mankind, their bite (of the female) often resulting in death, albeit it is decreasing study material.

However, what might be termed an unbiological situation is becoming more prevalent among the male black widows. More and more, the males are turning to each other for sexual gratification, in what would be termed homosexualism among the human species. The male spiders with palpi interlocked, as in a Japanese kendo match, is indeed an amazing sight.

Somebody once said, "Human nature has not changed since the first human." Likely spider nature has not changed since the first spider. But it is interesting to conjecture whether on some far distant tomorrow (1) the species will become extinct (like the great African scaled sloth which was too indolent to mate), (2) the female will see the error of her ways, and—superinduced by the dread of being a spinster—will adopt a police of "live and let live," or (3) the male will adroitly develop a "touch and go" procedure, leaving the female with murder in her heart as he rapidly departs after mating with an "it was fun while it lasted" attitude, or what passes for an attitude among spiders.

Perhaps some observer in 5000 A.B. (After the Atomic Bombing) will know the outcome of the erstwhile precarious love-life of the male black widow and the black pre-widow too.

"WELL, THAT'S A HELLUVA GODDAM NOTE! I WINE YOU, DINE YOU, BLOW FIFTY BUCKS ON FLOWERS AND TAXI FARE, AND NOW I FIND OUT YOU'RE CELIBATE!"

PETER SINCLAIR

"By 1975 sexual feeling and marriage will have nothing to do with each other."
—*John Langdon-Davies*

A little coitus never hoitus.

—*Anonymous*

DAMES MAKE THE MAN

ON HIS OWN, ARTEMUS THE PHLEGMY, HACKING ELEVATOR MAN, COULDN'T COMMAND THE ATTENTION OF A ROACH

Script: Josh Alan Friedman

BUT MATCH HIM UP WITH A HIGH-FALOOTIN' GOLDDIGGER AT THE COPA. EVERYONE WOULD THINK HE MUST BE THE CAT'S PAJAMAS.

MARCUS BOJOHNSON JR, NIGHT CUSTODIAN AT 1519 BROADWAY. COULDN'T GET SPIT UPON.

TH MOP IS MY MISTRESS

SLAP A TOP MODEL ON HIS ARM, WITH TWO TICKETS TO THE APOLLO -- PEOPLE MIGHT MISTAKE HIM FOR THE KING OF ETHIOPIA.

YOU'RE MY JANITORIAL DREAM.

ROTO-ROOTER MAN. GUS. SMELT SO BAD HOUSEWIVES RAN. BUT FOLKS WERE INTRIGUED WHEN HE BEGAN SHOWING UP ON CALLS BETWIXT A DUET OF HOT TAMALES.

AN' AWAY GO TROUBLES DOWN TH' DRAIN.

LIKEWISE, THE SECRETARIAL POOL DOWN AT THE OFFICE LOOKED AT JOE LIKE HE WAS SHIT. TILL THE DAY HE STROLLED IN WITH FIFI ON HIS ARM.

ON THE OTHER HAND, EVEN THE SHARPEST RACONTEUR MIGHT LOSE STATURE IF HE WERE SEEN IN THE WRONG COMPANY.

SO REMEMBER, GENT, WHEREVER YOU GO: *DAMES MAKE THE MAN!* END

eating mates

BY J. JORDAN CANNADY

It's a little past one in the morning and my wife and I are lying in bed reading. You can tell a lot about a person by examining the books that they read. On the small, cherry-wood end table by my side is my personal library. It consists of the following titles: *Silence of the Lamb*, *Dark Descent—a collection of Horror Stories*, *Fear and Loathing in Las Vegas*, and the text, *An Introduction To Language*. I have the entire spectrum of the horror genre represented—the psychopathic killer, the psychopathic journalist, and the psychopathic linguistic teacher.

On the other side of the arena are my wife's books: *English—The Mother Tongue*, *The Love Sonnets of John Donne*, and several scientific and scholarly tomes, books that would put me into a profound coma if I were to accidentally begin to read one. Not only does she read them, she takes enormous satisfaction in sharing passages from them with me. The closest I ever came to a genuine interest in the pursuit of scientific knowledge was when I went and asked Dr. Walters of the chemistry department at Tarleton State University what was it that caused Slimfast to get thick when you stirred it.

I don't want to know what the latest thinking is on the Kreb Cycle as it applies to the Derivation of the Clausius-Clapyron Equation. It bumfoozles and bewilders me to be drawn into a discussion about the Laffer Curve and it absolutely pisses me off to have my wife lean over to me and say, "You know, Jordan. Given the

> I had to admit that she'd piqued my interest, 'specially the be-heading connection.

paradoxical nature of the Heisenberg Uncertainty Principle, you may not have a world as you know it tomorrow or doesn't that bother you just a little?" It makes me want to lash out with a rolled up *Mad* magazine and strike her.

All of this leads up to a discussion we had the other evening about sex. Well, not so much about sex but about flies and sex. I was lying in bed watching Sally Jesse Raphael. It was a particularly intriguing episode that dealt with one of the more controversial subjects that face us today, "Dwarf Tossing." Sally had just brought out the first guest who said, "Hi, I'm Bob, and I toss dwarves." Sally was on her way out to the audience when my wife cleared her throat. I turned my head towards her and saw, to my dismay, that she held a book entitled *Dragons of Eden* by Carl Sagan. Having seen him on the Tonight Show several times I recognized the name Sagan as a scientist. I began to push myself up to escape when my wife grabbed my arm and attention.

"Jordan," she said as I strained at her grip. "You need to read this. It's the kind of stuff you like."

"What kind of stuff?" I asked, having been burned before.

"This whole section deals with sex and gratuitous violence, there's even some beheading in here. You'll definitely like this."

I had to admit that she'd piqued my interest, 'specially the beheading connection. I bit. "So what's it about?" Despite her efforts, on my behalf, to de-science the passage, I still got words like arthropods (bugs), olfactory (smell), and extirpation of the brain (what they do in the learning lab to prepare college freshmen for freshmen English). What follows is basically what she told me.

Sagan had observed that in certain species of insects, the female would bite the head off of her mate prior to intercourse. It seems that without a brain the male loses all sexual inhibitions and what's left of him performs sexually to her satisfaction. I told her that this was nothing startling. All she had to do was go down to Bostock's Bar and Grill to witness numerous examples of males getting well oiled, losing brain function, and then transforming into great hulking masses of raging hormones.

"Okay," she said. "Did you know that scientists have taken a male green bottle fly, snipped off his head, stuck it on a pin, and attached it with electrodes to an oscilloscope?"

I answered, "You think that's something? We used to give shots of Jose Cuervo Especial to my friend Dave Gunter's cat Jazbo and then take him to the zoo to see the kangaroos. So don't try to impress me with animal cruelty stories." I ducked my head as Sagan's book nearly creased my scalp.

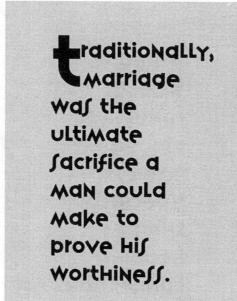

traditionally, marriage was the ultimate sacrifice a man could make to prove his worthiness.

"You didn't let me finish," she said. "After they've hooked him up, they passed a number of strong scents under his nose, ammonia, urea, British Sterling and others, but got no reaction. Next, they wafted some female green bottle fly pheromones under him and a line spiked on the oscilloscope. Isn't that interesting?"

Call me old fashioned. "Yes," I thought, "it was interesting." It was interesting that a group of Ph.D.s would sit around getting their ya-ya's off torturing flies.

Since that evening I've given some thought to the mating ritual. This in itself means nothing because most men spend a majority of their sentient hours thinking about that. I'm talking about mating on a higher, metaphysical level. What greater expression of love and devotion can one living creature make to another than to sacrifice his head?

Would the female praying mantis feel the same attraction for her mate if he said, "How about, for a change, I let you have one of my feet?"

I know, that in my case, having one of my size 12's lopped off at the ankle would make me *forget* my sexual inhibitions. I must confess that I have a pitifully low pain threshold and having my toe nails clipped a tad too short would probably have the same effect.

It's not the pain, but the long-term commitment that the female wants. After all, no matter how desperate a male is, giving up a head is a great deal more permanent than an apartment key.

So, if commitment is the key, how does a man go about demonstrating it? Traditionally, marriage was the ultimate sacrifice a man could make to prove his worthiness. This has changed. Now, with a career and identity of her own, the modern woman may not see a husband as much of a prize. There is nothing that a husband can provide or do for her that she can't find elsewhere: protection—she can buy a rottweiler; financial security—there are few jobs closed to women; companionship—there's always Bostocks.

There is little doubt in my mind that, as Dustin Hoffman once exclaimed in the movie *Rain Man*, "Grievous personal injury!" is the ticket. I'm not advocating offering his head on the chopping block. Extreme behavior is never good. Instead, I've searched the library and compiled a number of self-inflicted injuries that men may want to try in their attempts at seduction. The natives of Bora-Bora are quite keen on driving two-penny nails up their noses; in Bolivia and the Philippines self-flagellation using stinging nettles and scourges made out of flax is the rage; Tibetan men allow water buffalo to lie down upon their laps for hours; and in the Russian Ukraine the love-struck male will express his love by running head first into concrete walls. Here at home we smash cans against our foreheads, open glass bottles with our teeth, and plunge butt-naked into freezing ocean water on New Year's Day. It wasn't that many years ago that goldfish swallowing was considered an adequate demonstration of affection, and my Aunt Laura once told me about a love-crazed biology major at OSU who swallowed a six-foot long tape worm to prove his undying affection for her.

"Did it work?" I asked innocently.

"Go to hell, Jordan," she snapped back, her face flushing crimson. I knew then that it had.

I am married. The only time I'm obligated to suffer physically is when, once a year, I rip out a pound of my flesh and mail it to the IRS. While this is not intended as a means for achieving intercourse, the overall effect is the same. Each April, I picture some IRS form processor doing my form, firing up a cigarette and then sighing with pleasure.

For the single men out there who limp through life asking themselves what they're doing wrong, I suggest, invest in a handful of nails, find yourself a water buffalo, locate the nearest brick wall and lots of luck.

Only 35 and already Bob was experiencing
chest pains.

PETER SINCLAIR

ultimate nudity

(An excerpt from an interview with film director John Waters by E. J. Kahn III)

Interviewer: Is there anything that shocks you?
Waters: Yes—ultimate nudity. I heard about it in L. A. It's when you have the skin of your testicles removed and replaced with clear skin, the thinking being that it's more erotic to see how your body works inside. Think what will eventually happen: we'll all walk around with clear bodies, like high school science projects. "Oh, I can tell that person doesn't love me. His heart isn't beating fast." Or "I don't want to date that person. She drinks too much. Look at her liver." It's the ultimate voyeurism. I was shocked. But maybe that's the Nineties.

Condom Nations
standing up for the banana

(From an August 26 letter to Bruce Christensen, president of PBS, from Robert M. Moore, president of the International Banana Association. Moore is writing to protest a program on AIDS scheduled for broadcast on WETA, a Washington, D.C. public-television station.)

Dear Mr. Christensen,

In this program, a banana is used as a substitute for a human penis in a demonstration of how condoms should be used.

I must tell you, Mr. Christensen, as I have told representatives of WETA, that our industry finds such usage of our product to be totally unacceptable. The choice of a banana rather than some other inanimate prop constitutes arbitrary and reckless disregard for the unsavory association that will be drawn by the public and the damage to our industry that will result therefrom.

The banana is an important product and deserves to be treated with respect and consideration. It is the most extensively consumed fruit in the United States, being purchased by over 98 percent of households. It is important to the economies of many developing Latin American nations. The banana's continued image in the minds of consumers as a healthful and nutritious product is critically important to the industry's continued ability to be held in such high regard by the public and to discharge its responsibilities to its Latin American hosts.

Unfortunately, WETA categorically refused my request to view the offensive sequence, citing policies established by PBS.

Mr. Christensen, I have no alternative but to advise you that we intend to hold PBS fully responsible for any and all damages sustained by our industry as a result of the showing of this AIDS program depicting the banana in the associational context planned. Further, we reserve all legal rights to protect the industry's interests from this arbitrary, unnecessary, and insensitive action.

Yours very truly,
Robert M. Moore

What Love is

COMPILED BY NEIL GENZLINGER

Love Is a Milkweed Pot (1903)
Love Is Like a Dizziness (1905)
Love Is as Old as the World, Dear (1910)
Love Is Like a Shoogy Shoo (1912)
Love Is a Sickness Full of Woes (1912)
Love Is a Babe (1919)
Love Is Sunshine, Not Moonshine (1919)
Love Is an I.O.U. (1925)
Love Is Like the Influenza (1927)
Love Is Coy and Wanton (1928)
Love Is My Radio Station (1931)
Love Is Good for Anything That Ails You (1936)
Love Is Something Like Photography (1937)
Love Is on a Sit-down Strike (1937)
Love Is a Dimpling Doodle Bug (1943)
Love Is a Traitor (1944)
Love Is a Game for Soldiers (1945)
Love Is Doggone Mean (1947)
Love Is Your Prescription (1947)
Love Is a Cigarette (1947)
Love Is Atomic (1950)
Love Is a Cocktail (1951)
Love Is a Dirty Spoon (1951)

Love Is a Glass of Champagne (1952)
Love Is on the Ten-Yard Line (1953)
Love Is a Whip (1955)
Love Is Orbiting Around Me (1959)
Love Is a Bore (1964)
Love Is Hell in a Small Hotel (1966)
Love Is a Miniskirted Thing (1968)
Love Is Psychedelic (1968)
Love Is Groovy (1969)
Love Is Not One Color, Child (1970)
Love Is a Nickel Bag (1970)
Love Is a Three-Letter Word
Love Is Like a Hydrant (1972)
Love Is a Heavy Number (1973)
Love Is a Cannibal (1973)
Love Is a Four-Letter Word (1975)
Love Is a Five-Letter Word (1975)
Love Is a Funky Thing (1976)
Love Is Suicide (1979)
Love Is So Good When You're Stealing It (1987)
Love Is Mercenary (1988)
Love Is a Loaded Gun (1988)
Love Is for Suckers (1988)

Heretoforeplay
the consensual sex contract

By The National Center for Men

Agreement before lovemaking entered into by _____ and _____, this ____ day of _____, 199_.

Whereas, the parties to this agreement want to be sexually intimate, but also want to avoid the misunderstandings that sometimes occur after sex,

Now, therefore, the parties enter into the following agreements (check one declaration from each pair):

___ We want to have a relationship that may lead to sexual intercourse.
___ We want to have sex but without intercourse.

___ We want to have sex as a way of expressing an emotional commitment that may eventually lead to marriage.
___ We want to have a sexual relationship but we're not ready for marriage.

___ We want our relationship to be monogamous.
___ We both want the freedom to see other people.

___ We want to have sex in order to conceive a child.
___ We're not ready to be parents now. If an unplanned pregnancy occurs, neither one of us will try to force the other into parenthood.

___ We want our sexual encounter to be discreet.
___ We want the whole world to know about our love for each other.

Neither of us may claim to be the victim of sexual harassment or assault or rape as a result of the acts which are the subject of this agreement. By signing this contract, we acknowledge that the anticipated sexual experience will be of mutual consent.

We understand that this contract may be terminated at any time by either one of us *except* during the sexual activity contemplated by this agreement.

We understand that no provision of this agreement relieves us of the obligations to treat each other with caring and mutual respect.

In witness thereof, the parties execute the aforementioned agreement.

_____   _____
(Man's signature)   *(Woman's signature)*

fowl display

(from a memo sent by National Convenience Stores, a Houston-based retail chain, to all of its store managers.)

We have received a number of complaints on the Rubber Ducky Condoms. The package (which pictures a rubber duck, the company's logo) appears to be misleading, and customers have complained that these condoms are being displayed with the toys or in the candy section.

Any store that carries this product is requested to check the location where this inventory is displayed. For those stores who have these condoms merchandised in the candy section or with the toys, you need to remove them immediately and merchandise this product only in the health-and-beauty-aids section next to the other brands of condoms.

Your cooperation in this matter is appreciated. If you have any questions, please contact your district manager.

A sufi tale

One afternoon Nasruddin and his friend were in a cafe drinking tea, and talking about life and love.

"How come you never got married, Nasruddin?" asked his friend at one point.

"Well," said Nasruddin, "to tell you the truth, I spent my youth looking for the perfect woman. In Cairo, I met a beautiful and intelligent woman, with eyes like dark olives, but she was unkind. Then in Baghdad, I met a woman who was a wonderful and generous soul, but we had no interests in common. One woman after another would seem just right, but there would always be something missing. Then one day I met her. She was beautiful, intelligent, generous and kind. We had everything in common. In fact, she was perfect."

"Well," said Nasruddin's friend, "What happened? Why didn't you marry her?"

Nasruddin sipped his tea reflectively. "Well," he replied, "it's a sad thing; seems she was looking for the perfect man."

"HOW MUCH WOULD YOU GIVE ME FOR THE CAR IF I THROW IN ONE USED HUSBAND?"

the 51st Way to Leave Your Lover
relax, breathe, visualize, dump her

BY GERALD EPSTEIN, M.D.

In my practice I often encounter the suffering experienced in not being able to end a relationship. Here is one tried-and-true way to accomplish this:

Exercise: Parting and Departing
Intention: To end the influence of a person in your life; to end a relationship
Frequency: Each morning for three to five minutes, for seven days

Close your eyes. Breathe in and out three times and see yourself on a beach. The one with whom you wish to end the relationship is lying there. You have with you golden ropes with lead weights at the ends. With these you truss up your "friend." There is a large rowboat nearby. Put your "friend" in the boat and row out to the deepest spots in the world. Stand up in the boat, lift your "friend's" trussed-up body, and toss it overboard, knowing that you are *ridding yourself of the influence of* that person. Watch the body disappear as it sinks, forming a small whirlpool. Know that it is going to the bottom, never to resurface. After it has gone out of sight, sit down in the boat and row back to shore with a new feeling and attitude about yourself. When you reach the shore, stow the oars and beach the boat, and return to your home alone. Then open your eyes.

"Our marriage counselor always liked you best."

Let the Men of Wisdom Speak

My schoolmates would make love to anything that moved, but I never saw any reason to limit myself.

—Emo Phillips

Sex is good, but not as good as fresh sweetcorn.

—Garrison Keillor

"Nothing is so prone to contaminate—under certain circumstances, even to exhaust—the source of all noble and ideal sentiments...as the practice of masturbation in early years."

—Richard Freiherr von Krafft-Ebing

I was the best I ever had.

—Woody Allen

"I am so tired of all this talk about "straight" and "gay." You cannot separate men into two camps, "straight" and "gay." That's just an effort to divide and weaken men. The truth is, there are two kinds of men: men who look good in a tank top and men who don't. And the ones who do are insufferable."

—Roy Blount, Jr.

"Some people have big ones; some people have little ones. Women have been shorted on them. Nobody really wants to know—but, on the other hand, everybody does want to know how his stacks up next to the other fellow's. It's not so much the size of them as what you do with them and what goes along with them. (Sure!) There is a taboo against revealing them....Salaries."

—Roy Blount, Jr.

After learning that natives drank the blood of their enemies to surpass them in strength, Bob guzzles his girlfriend's nail polish.

hickerson

"AFTER 30 YEARS OF MARRIAGE, WE BOTH RETIRED FROM OUR CAREERS AND FOUND OUT WE CAN'T STAND EACH OTHER."

My Life With the M.O.B.

BY J. JORDAN CANNADY

Warning: This contains material that mothers of brides will find offensive. Ladies, do not read this. You will not be amused.

Do you *like* weddings? Do your eyes mist and does your throat tighten as the groom and groomette exchange bands of gold, kiss like a pair of Puritans, turn and run the gauntlet of forced smiles, pawing hands and flying rice? Do you cheer as the couple pulls away from the curb in their chariot with its shoe-polish war paint and cacophonous trail of cans and shoes?

Or—like me—do you hate weddings?

Not everything about a wedding is hateful, just certain aspects. Wedding dresses, for example.

In Dear Abby's column a letter writer mentioned a wedding dress with a $14,000 price tag. Taking into account the financial condition of the world, $14,000 seems a tad excessive.

That kind of money, after all, will buy a nice car, put a child through college, support an entire village in Bora Bora or pay my yearly veterinarian's bill.

Perhaps we should change the standard. How about the top-of-the-line wedding dress in Georgia-Pacific's paper wedding dress line, "The Scarlet O'Hara" at only $59.95.

Not only is the dress lovely, it's functional. Imagine the joy the couple will feel on each anniversary as they sift it out (folded and pressed!) from inside of the wedding album and gaze upon it fondly.

On their 50th wedding anniversary, it could be unfolded and used as a drop-cloth under the punch bowl. At a little over a dollar a year, it would be the finest investment in their lives together.

The mother of the bride (MOB) can spend more energy tracking down nail polish in just the right shade of avocado blush to match the bride's shoes, than the Center for Disease Control in Atlanta does finding a cure for the latest flu bug.

Are we to believe that the groom cares? His darling bride could be barefoot and he wouldn't notice!

This brings us to the cold, hard truth about weddings. Like kelp that drifts in the tide, the groom is really a non-essential participant in THE WEDDING.

True, he must be there; society is not yet ready to accept proxy grooms. But from the cut of his hair, to the flavor of his own groom's cake, the MOB has ultimate control.

Left up to the grooms of the world (which it isn't and never will be), weddings would be come-as-you-are, three-minute rituals held in auto part stores.

Face it: Deep down, most men are shallow. It's for our own benefit, it would seem, that the MOB is there to steer our romances. Were it not for the MOB, where would all those dressmakers, cakemakers, rice farmers, photographers, garter manufacturers and florists go?

There are those, of course, who will insist that any criticisms of the wedding ceremony are only a thin veil over a bad attitude concerning the institution of marriage.

Nothing could be further from the truth. Wasn't it Plato who once said, "He who laughs at the ceremonial trappings that guide our lives will live to be a wise man?"

I don't know if he said it, but incorporating a little Greek wisdom on my side may keep me out of the dog house another week.

"Talk about mixed emotions! I just caught
my wife in bed with my girlfriend!"

Major credibility problems on Mt. Olympus.

divorce, American style

During his divorce from actress Joan Collins, Peter Holm filed the following monthly expenses in support of his request for $80,000/month spousal support.

Exhibit A

The following estimates of my present monthly expenses are based on actual expenses for the calendar year 1986.

Projected new residence:		Other:	
Rent	$16,500.00	Club Membership and Dues	400.00
Household Salaries	7,000.00	Newspapers and Magazines	100.00
Payroll Taxes	1,400.00	Personal Grooming	200.00
Household Cash	300.00	Medical Expenses	250.00
Household Supplies		Gifts	1,650.00
General	700.00	Audio Supplies	400.00
Groceries	1,900.00	Computer Equipment and Supplies	3,000.00
Hardware, etc	200.00	Freight and Messengers	100.00
Miscellaneous	500.00	Office Expenses	1,125.00
Maintenance	500.00	Books	280.00
Utilities	600.00	Clothing and Accessories	12,000.00
Telephone	1,300.00	Photos and Supplies	800.00
TV Cable and Video Supplies	670.00	Subscriptions	36.00
Dry Cleaning	100.00	Maintenance and Taxes	
Insurance	300.00	(Port Grimaud)	1,500.00
Security—Bel Air Patrol	200.00	Advertising	250.00
TOTAL:	32,170.00	Entertainment	6,000.00
Car expenses:		Cash Draws	8,000.00
Leasing of 1984 BMW	3,910.00	Travel and Lodging	4,000.00
Gas	160.00	Limousine Expenses	500.00
Repairs and Maintenance	1,300.00	TOTAL:	40,591.00
Depreciation	1,500.00	GRAND TOTAL:	$80,056.00
Insurance	400.00		
Registration	25.00		
TOTAL:	7,295.00		

Petitioned and hidden from me despite the court order of February 17, 1987, which stated that I should have exclusive, temporary use of my BMW 635CS1. In order to maintain properly both vehicles, the cost is approximately $2,800 per month, due to their luxury nature.

During our marriage we purchased a second family home, located at 1196 Cabrillo Drive, Beverly Hills, for $1,950,000 cash, which we paid for with some funds earned during our marriage. The home comprises 13,000 square feet of living space, including a huge master bedroom suite, a separate guest house, and numerous other amenities—including room to park twenty cars, a large pool and fountains, an extensive lawn, and terraced walks throughout the estate.

In order to maintain my current life style I have begun looking for a permanent residence in the area. I realize that to live in a property like the Cabrillo residence may be unrealistic for me at this time. However, I have looked at residences about half the size of the Cabrillo property that would be suitable to me and find that the monthly rent is $16,500.

Throughout our marriage I have dressed stylishly. I have spent large sums updating my wardrobe to enhance my wife's and my public image. I spent approximately $20,000 per month on clothing and accessories. I purchased an extensive amount of clothing while I traveled (always first class) in Europe during our marriage. In fact, during our marriage we withdrew over $600,000 in cash for these kinds of expenditures.

Shopping was one of our favorite pastimes and we patronized such places as *Rodeo Drive* in Beverly Hills. We both have expensive tastes in our choice of wardrobes. Our life style demands that we wear quality clothing at all times, including expensive leather and fur jackets, ties, watches, shoes, and silk shirts. For instance, I wear $2,000 leather jackets, $400 crocodile shoes, and tens of thousands of dollars worth of jewelry.

While our income and expenses may seem extraordinary to the average person, the fact of the matter is that to us it is our normal way of life and is typical of those depicted in the television series *Lifestyles of the Rich and Famous*, on which we have been featured several times.

Because I am presently unemployed, and all savings during the marriage were invested in our Cabrillo home, my cash flow is, at present, zero. Therefore, I am requesting $80,000 per month *pendente lite* support in order that I can maintain my standard of living which I have enjoyed previous to and during our marriage. Petitioner's income is more than sufficient to support my request for temporary support while maintaining her life style and standard of living.

MeN at Work, MeN at Play

FRED
SMITH
1944 - 1992
"A LITTLE
HARD WORK
NEVER HURT
ANYBODY"

P.S.

P. S. MUELLER

"I'M WORRIED ABOUT MR. SLOAN. I THINK HE'S BEEN IN THE RAT RACE TOO LONG."

"I'm sensing confidence, boldness and moral sensibility.
You're not going to turn out to be a whistle-blower are you?"

Love my job! Work is fun!
reflections of a rivethead

By Ben Hamper

It's in the vicinity of last call and I'm propped up next to the Beer Nuts display in Mark's Lounge. Someone keeps playin' "The Heat Is On" by Glenn Frey. I hate Glenn Frey. I hate him and all the rest of the Eagles.

All around me are the sounds of my co-workers yapping it up and tossing 'em down. We descend on this tavern nightly—clutching our paroles, maddened with thirst, looking for any good reason to laugh at ourselves. We don't need Glenn Frey advising us on the heat. It's hot, we realize. It's hotter than a cobra's dick. It's all brains afire and radioactive crotches and smoldering men piled high at the waterhole. That old factory labor in the middle of July is all you'll ever need to greet the heat. What gets most of through is the knowledge that when it's all over there will be several tall cold ones aimed straight for the windpipe.

Up strolls a guy from the truck plant in a "Mark's Lounge" softball jacket. I hate softball. "You've gotta tell 'em about the barbed wire," he says. This guy routinely mistakes me for a writer. I believe he's seen my name printed somewhere. "You've gotta get that in your paper. Tell 'em about the goddamned barbed wire." I give a slow nod. "They should know," I reply. This always seems to make him feel better.

As long as I've know this man, the only topic we've ever discussed is the barbed wire fence that surrounds the truck plant. Plainly, it must annoy the hell outta him. Others moan about the overtime or the boredom or the rotten humidity, but with this guy, the conversation never varies. Always the barbed wire. "It doesn't make any sense," he will say. "The barbed wire all faces in. The shit's pointed right down our throats. They don't want to keep others out, they wanta *keep us* in!"

He's right, of course. And here I'd always figured that the barbed wire was just so much precautionary neckware strung around the grounds to ward off would-be Empire looters. Just the Corporation's paranoid way of pissing on its boundaries. You never know who might try to drop by and pilfer the cookbook.

Silly me. Just one look will tell you that GM must have designed their security fencing with one guarded eyeball on their own work force. Maybe they believe we're all double agents—plotting to swap the recipe for our cherished Chevy Blazer military vehicle with a carload of Russians parked on the dark side of the train yard. The ingredients of Ronnie's new Death Wagons, even up for ten cases of Stroh's.

Maybe they live in fear that one hot August night we'll be smitten with road fever and roam our bunions elsewhere. We'll all toss down our gloves, rub axle grease on our faces, load up our coolers fulla car stereos and carburetors, and flee over the west wall. "Warning! We Command You Rivetheads to Halt!" (the shriek of gunfire and Glenn Frey records). "Halt Immediately or No More Microwave Popcorn for Six Months!!!"

Maybe there's nothing to it at all. Maybe GM strung up all this confounding barbed wire just to give us Midnight Plowboys something to chew on in between the Beer Nuts and the swizzle sticks, the long wait for death and the heat to go off.

I must tell you about the mammoth electronic message board they've positioned right next to me at my job. I'm sure that someday soon it will drive me completely mad.

The message board hangs about twenty feet away from me and blinks all day and all night long. GM sprang for only ten of these boards, and wouldn't you know it, with all of the acreage they have around this place, they just had to point one right at me. The messages range from corny propaganda to motivational pep talks. From birthday salutes to abstract gibberish. (One day, the board kept flashing the phrase "Happiness Is Horses." Alongside the phrase was a large computer rendering of a horse's head. If I knew what it all meant, I would tell you.)

The first day the board went into operation it flashed one single message the entire shift. They never erased it. It was there when I arrived and it was there when I left at 2:00 A.M. The message? Get ready, theologians: "Squeezing Rivets Is Fun!" Can you believe it?

Imagine you worked for the sewage department and they erected a giant neon sign right next to you that blinked nothing but "Shoveling Turds Is Fun." Or that you were a shoe clerk and you were forced to stare all day at a ten-foot billboard insisting "Smelling Feet Is Rapture." What would you do? I know what I did. I cut me up a hunk of cardboard, took a red crayon, and etched

down the letters "cked." Then I crammed a bunch of tape to the back of my creation, stood on the workers' picnic bench, and slapped those four letters over the "n" in "fun." I'm a stickler for accuracy. My proud correction stayed up there for about three hours, until a guy in a tie ripped it down amid a chorus of boos.

Now listen, GM. I have a fair idea of what I think is fun. Taking in a ball game is fun. Behaving like an idiot is fun. Having sex in a Subaru. That's fun, too. Squeezing rivets is *not* fun. It pays the rent and keeps Fritos in our children's bellies but in no way, shape, or form is it *fun*. Not even a little. Not yesterday, not today, not tomorrow.

I think next time GM should go right to the source for their information. I'm available weekdays from 4:30 till closing. I work next to a guy with a rodent tattooed on his arm. I install dual-exhaust muffler hangers and hit tons of rivets. I wear blue T-shirts and am losing some hair.

If you come by, I will teach you my job. Then I will go across the street to Mark's Lounge. I will pull up a chair at the end of the bar. I will order a Bud and drink it slowly. It will be fun.

B.C. by Johnny Hart

PETER SINCLAIR

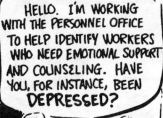

PETER SINCLAIR

"REMEMBER, BOB, IT'S NOT HOW YOU PLAY THE GAME -- IT'S IF YOU WIN OR LOSE THAT COUNTS!"

Attila the Hun, a ground-breaking pioneer in progressive personnel management.

DONNING THE TRIBAL MASKS OF POWER, REDFORD LEWIS, SHAMANIC CEO, LEADS THE FIRM IN A DANCE FOR WEALTH + PROSPERITY.

PETER SINCLAIR

PETER SINCLAIR

Tsai Chih Chung

BECOMING ONE WITH THE DOW

OFF THE DEEP END ©1989 Andrew Lehman-concept by Bill Montgomery

I'M SO FED UP WITH MY JOB! IT'S LIKE, MY BOSS THINKS HE **OWNS** ME!

WELL THIS IS ONE GUY THAT CAN'T BE **BOUGHT!**

SINCLAIR

BUT, HAVEN'T YOU BEEN DOING THAT JOB FOR FIFTEEN YEARS NOW?

LEASED! NOT BOUGHT!

WOW,... I WORKED TOO MANY HOURS LAST WEEK!

YOU KNOW, CIVILIZED MAN HASN'T MADE MUCH PROGRESS ON THAT.

12-10

FOR INSTANCE, THE ABORIGINAL BUSHMEN NEEDED ONLY 12 TO 20 HOURS A WEEK TO PROVIDE FOR THEIR NEEDS!

WOW! REALLY?

SINCLAIR

HOW MUCH DID THEY MAKE AN HOUR?

I HAVE TO THINK OF AN ACTIVITY FOR THE ANNUAL COMPANY OUTING!

THE LAST FEW YEARS THEY'VE DONE ALL THESE ARDUOUS, ADVENTUROUS SORT OF THINGS TO DEVELOP GROUP IDENTITY AND BONDING.

FIRST, IT WAS RIVER RAFTING, THEN IT WAS ROCK CLIMBING, AND THEN LAST YEAR IT WAS FIRE WALKING!

SO, I NEED SOMETHING THAT'S SORT OF AN **ORDEAL**, THAT WE CAN ALL PARTICIPATE IN TO BUILD DISCIPLINE, TO REALLY **MARK** US AS A TEAM!

WHY NOT JUST BRAND 'EM ALL WITH THE COMPANY LOGO?

THAT'S GREAT! IT'S **UNIQUE!!** WE COULD DO THAT!!...

PETER SINCLAIR

I can't believe THIS! I come home from a hard day's work hoping to find a clean house and dinner on the table and what do I find out?...I'm still SINGLE!!
hickerson

Bob Quigman: The Fodder of Our Country.

"I hate this job. The retirement plan really bites."

PETER SINCLAIR

DRUMMING WORKSHOP

PETER SINCLAIR

DANCE WORKSHOP

PETER SINCLAIR

AIR GUITAR WORKSHOP

"SO I FIGURED, WHY NOT PICK UP SOME EXTRA BUCKS WHILE I'M JOGGING?"

King Solomon's pollster

© BRADFORD VELEY

"Your order is not ready, nor will it ever be."

"Come along, Caswell; we have a new slot for you down in marketing."

"Insofar as hard figures are still unavailable, our Mr. Rendleman has written a poem which explores the essence of the firms situation."

"I'm obliged to warn you that I am a Master of Business Administration!"

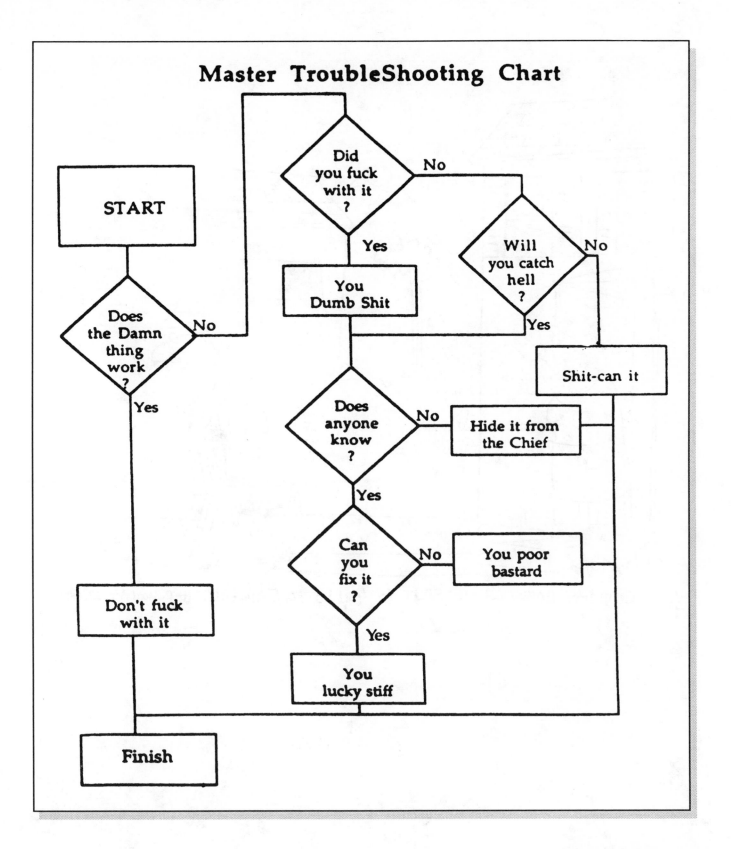

Master TroubleShooting Chart

START

Does the Damn thing work?

No → Did you fuck with it?

No → Will you catch hell?

No → Shit-can it

Yes → You Dumb Shit

Yes → Does anyone know?

No → Hide it from the Chief

Yes → Can you fix it?

No → You poor bastard

Yes → You lucky stiff

Yes → Don't fuck with it

Finish

"HAVE A GOOD DAY DOING WHATEVER IT IS YOU DO TO EARN ALL THAT MOOLAH, REGINALD."

the tao of baseball

BY PETER GARDELLA

Baseball diamonds organize space in much the same way as the basilica of St. Peter at Rome, the altar of heaven at Peking, and the great mosque at Mecca. What happens on a baseball diamond may seem to be only a sport, but the pattern of the field and the rules of the game also form a ritual.

To look at a baseball diamond, as millions of Americans do for billions of hours every summer, is to contemplate a mandala: a design that aids meditation by drawing attention from its borders toward its center. Within every baseball diamond is a mound of earth, a circle marking the center of a square, to which the focus of the game returns with every pitch. Like the burial mounds of Native Americans, the stupas of Theravadin Buddhists, and the earth altars of Hindus, the pitcher's mound is an especially sacred space.

Of course, within the base lines all space is sacred; it is "fair" territory, as opposed to the "foul" territory of spectators and reserves. There are borders around the playing fields of all sports. But unlike other fields, and like the great mandalas at Mecca and at Rome, a baseball diamond organizes the whole world. The foul lines go on forever, so that a ball hit over the fence, out of the stadium, or 10,000 miles away could still be fair. Every home plate is the center of the earth, where the quarter of the world that is fair territory meets the three-quarters of the world that is foul.

As a player moves from home to first base, to second, to third, and then home again, the succession of states of consciousness suggests the life cycle. A player is most alert while batting. At first base the player accepts congratulations and turns into a base runner, still with many decisions to make but also at the mercy of the batter. At second the runner relaxes a bit more and usually gives up any thought of stealing. On third there

is almost no chance of independent action; the runner stands in foul territory and waits to be brought home. The journey ends with a return into the earth, down the steps of the dugout.

Fours and threes, the basic units of religious numerology, also inform the ritual of baseball. As Carl Jung pointed out, threes everywhere stand for abstract perfection: the Trinity of Christians and of Plato, the nine steps between each of the three levels in the Chinese altar of heaven. Fours mean completeness, as in the four elements of ancient science. In baseball, every number that concerns abstract perfection—the three strikes per batter and the three outs per inning, the nine defensive players, the unbroken string of twenty-seven outs over nine innings in a "perfect" game— is a three or a multiple of three. Only when a fourth is added, when the player walks on four balls or circles all four bases to score a run, does anything actually happen.

Adding four to three makes seven, the number of creation. And just as God reached the seventh day and rested, so the baseball fan stands up and stretches in the seventh inning.

What Martin Buber said of religious ritual is also true of baseball: the game is not in time, but time is in the game. Whether ten minutes or half an hour has passed has no more relevance to a baseball game than to a Mass or a wedding. Twenty-seven outs for both teams is the standard length of a game, but there are several ways, in theory, for the game to go on forever: by an excess of batting skill, by perfect pitching, or by perfect balance between the teams. In fact, a player's time at bat can last forever if he keeps on hitting foul balls. No other game is so open to infinity. As Yogi Berra said, "It ain't over till it's over."

The mention of Yogi Berra brings to mind another similarity between baseball and Eastern religions. Hitting a pitched ball demands such unclouded vision, immediate judgment, and precise coordination that one can hit well only in a state of mind Buddhists might call *samadhi*, a state of naked awareness, of wakefulness without a single thought. if a hitter has this awareness, neither excess weight nor lack of speed matters. Witness the facial and bodily resemblance of Babe Ruth to Gautama Sakyamuni, whose samadhi caused people to call him "the one who woke up," or the Buddha.

A mathematician named Hall
Has a hexahedronical ball.
    And the cube of its weight
      Times his pecker, plus eight,
Is his phone number—give him a call.

the ties that bind

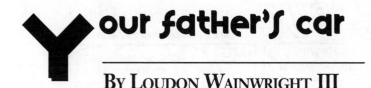

Your father's car

By Loudon Wainwright III

When you borrow your father's car
Doesn't matter how old you are
You don't ever drive too far
When you borrow your father's car

And when you drink at your mother's house
Have a couple but don't get soused
You don't want to play surrogate spouse
(with her)
When you drink at your mother's house

You don't wanna make the old man boil
The jalopy needs the treatment royal
Play it safe every time and check the oil
You don't wanna make the old man boil

When your kids come to spend a weekend
And more and more that is
Becoming the trend
Get rid of the new girl friend ('til Monday)
When your kids come to spend the weekend

And if you're napping on your ex's futon
Oh you know that's not where you belong
When you notice some new stains thereon
when you're napping on your ex's futon

(Because) if you're travelling out of state
Don't forget to check the license plate
I mean the sticker expiration date
When you're travelling out of state

© 1989 Snowden Music, Inc.

"Football little league is getting to be a drag but my dad gets such a kick out of participating, I hate to quit and disappoint him."

"Before I tell you the facts of life, let
me tell you the myths of marriage."

It's a dad's life

AT TWO·AND·A·HALF A CHILD IS VERY INQUISITIVE. I MAKE EVERY EFFORT TO ANSWER ALL HIS QUESTIONS.

IT'S KIND OF COOL IN HERE TODAY, ISN'T IT...

WHY?

WELL, BECAUSE THE SEASONS ARE CHANGING, I GUESS, AND FALL IS COMING...

WHY?

WELL, BECAUSE THE EARTH'S AXIS IS TILT

WHY?

BECAUSE ACCORDING TO THE BIG BANG THEORY, PARTIC

WHY?

SOME CHILDREN GET THE HANG OF POTTY·TRAINING SOONER THAN OTHERS. ONE DAY, AFTER WE HAD EXPLAINED IT EXHAUSTIVELY, DYLAN PROUDLY ANNOUNCED THAT HE HAD 'PUT SOMEPING IN POTTY.'

HE HAD: FOURTEEN TRUCKS.

JIM BORGMAN

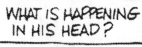

WHAT IS HAPPENING IN HIS HEAD?

I OFTEN WONDER WHAT A DAY LOOKS LIKE TO DYLAN, HOW HE CONCEIVES IT.

Monday June 16
8:15 Red dumptrucks
8:30 Cheerios
8:45 Pick up stones
9:00 Stop on each step
9:15 Think about garage doors
9:30 Ask about them 84 times
9:45 Blue things
10:00 Be a rhino
10:15 Ask unintelligible question
10:30 Destroy living room

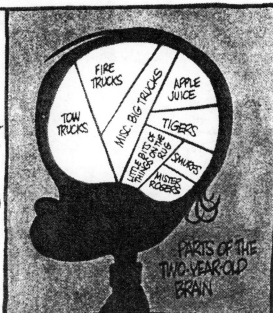

PARTS OF THE TWO-YEAR-OLD BRAIN

FIRE TRUCKS
TOW TRUCKS
MISC. BIG TRUCKS
APPLE JUICE
TIGERS
LITTLE BITS OF STUFF ON THE RUG
SHARKS
MISTER ROGERS

CHRISTMAS TREE STILL GONE, MOMMY!!!!

YOU CAN BE REASONABLY CERTAIN A HUMAN BEING IS TWO YEARS OLD BY HIS ENDLESS FASCINATION WITH A SINGLE FACT.

IT IS AN AWESOME EXPERIENCE TO FIND ONESELF IN THE PRESENCE OF A SUDDEN AND UNPROVOKED WORD SPILL.

BIG MONKEY 'N' GIRAFFE TALL NECK 'N' ELPHINTS 'N' BIG TRUNK 'N' CLOWNS N' GO BOOM! FALL DOWN 'N' SHARKS! ROWR SCARY 'N' BIG TEETH AND SIRENS GO FAST! BLANKETS 'N' BANG 'I' FUNNY MISROGERS SWEATE PEANU RANDMA ROUND AND ROUND

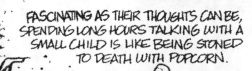

FASCINATING AS THEIR THOUGHTS CAN BE, SPENDING LONG HOURS TALKING WITH A SMALL CHILD IS LIKE BEING STONED TO DEATH WITH POPCORN.

JIM BORGMAN

"...so then Father Flannegan says to the Judge: 'There are no bad boys — only guilty parents!'."

Having a family is like having a bowling alley installed in your brain.

—*Martin Mull*

I had dinner with my father last night, and I made a classic Freudian slip. I meant to say, "Please pass the salt," but it came out, "You prick, you ruined my childhood."

—*Jonathan Katz*

My daughter has me totally wrapped around her little finger. I don't even try to win anymore. I just try and save face. I say things to her like, "Go to your room at your earliest convenience. O.K. Daddy's going to count to fifteen hundred."

—*Jonathan Katz*

PETER SINCLAIR

contributors

Sherman Alexie is a Spokane/Coeur d'Alene Indian and the author *The Business of Fancy Dancing*, a collection of stories and poems.

Aaron Bacall is a cartoonist living in Staten Island, New York.

Dave Barry is a Pulitzer Prize-winning columnist with the *Miami Herald*. He has several best sellers to his credit including *Dave Barry Looks at 40*.

Steve Bhaerman, aka Swami Beyondananda, makes his home in Austin, Texas.

John Boni has written extensively for all media. His television credits include such sitcoms as "Three's Company," "Facts of Life" and "227." He has created a long-running, syndicated sitcom titled "Out of This World" and co-created with Mel Brooks a spoof of Robin Hood for ABC TV called "When Things Were Rotten." He was co-head writer of the cult classic "Fernwood 2Nite" and "America 2Nite" which starred Martin Mull and Fred Willard. He lives in Encino, California, with his wife and three children.

Jim Borgman, a Pulitzer winning political cartoonist, lives in Cincinnati, and draws for the *Cincinnati Enquirer*.

Art Bouthillier has been freelancing to major magazines since 1983. He currently resides in an old summer cabin overlooking the killer whale infested waters of Puget Sound on beautiful Whidbey Island, Washington. His roommates include his girlfriend, two Doberman Pinchers, and three cats, adding up to countless cartoon ideas.

Berke Breathed is the Pulitzer Prize winner for his cartoon "Bloom County." He currently produces "Outland" from his home in Seattle.

Joe Bob Briggs is the alter ego of John Bloom, an actor, comedian, and satirist. He has written six books of humor, criticism and journalism, including his most recent book, *Iron Joe Bob*. He was born in Dallas, grew up in Little Rock, Arkansas, attended Vanderbilt University, and now lives in New York City.

John Callahan is the author of an illustrated autobiography, *Don't Worry, He Won't Get Far On Foot* and two cartoon collections, *Do Not Disturb Any Further* and *Digesting the Child Within*, and a forthcoming collection, *Do What He Says, He's Crazy*. His cartoons appear in several newspapers and magazines, and he has been the subject of feature articles in the *New York Times* and *Los Angeles Times* as well a recent "60 Minutes" feature. He lives in Portland, Oregon.

J. Jordan Cannaday is a native born Texan living in Stephenville, Texas, with his wife and teenage daughter, which accounts for his admittedly twisted outlook on life. He has had over 150 cartoons and over 75 articles published in various newspapers and magazines including the *Dallas Morning News*.

Tsai Chih Chung is an immensely popular Taiwanese cartoonist whose characters entertain Chinese readers all over the world.

Samuel Clemens, aka Mark Twain, died during the 1910 appearance of Halley's Comet.

Franklin Crawford writes for the *Ithaca Journal* in Upstate New York.

Chip Dunham's syndicated strip "Overboard" appears in 100 papers through Universal Press. He lives in Michigan.

Tim Eagan has been drawing "Subconscious Comics" since 1981. In 1991 he published *The Collected Subconscious*, an anthology of his weekly cartoon strip. His political cartoons and illustrations appear in the *San Francisco Examiner* and several other publications. He has also produced two comic books, *All Night Comics* and *All Night Comics #2*. He lives and works in Santa Cruz, California.

Gerald Epstein is the author of *Healing Visualizations*.

Jules Feiffer's work can be seen in several newspapers and magazines.

Ken Fisher, aka Ruben Bollings, creates the comic strip "Tom the Dancing Bug" which is distributed by Quaternary Features. His first book is also titled *Tom the Dancing Bug*.

Drew Friedman was born in New York City back in the fifties and for some reason remains there today. His comics and illustrations appear in publications such as *Raw*, *Weirdo*, *Blab*, *National Lampoon*, *The Village Voice* and *Spy*, where he contributes a monthly feature. His other credits include his first book, *Any Similarities to Persons Living or Dead*, illustrations for *News of the Weird* and his romantic homage to New York, *Tales of Times Square*. He is also a musician performing as Josh Alan with a solo album forthcoming to coincide with the release of his third book, *Warts*. He lives in New York City with his wife Kathy and three cats.

Peter Gardella is an Associate Professor of Religion. He has written the book *Innocent Ecstasy: How Christianity Gave America an Ethic of Sexual Pleasure*. He lives in Hamden, Connecticut, with his wife and seven-year old son.

Bud Grace has a Ph.D. in Physics. His cartoon strip "Ernie" is syndicated nationally by King Features.

Lewis Grizzard is a humorist with the *Atlanta Journal*. Several of his books have been best sellers including *Chili Dawgs Only Bark at Night*.

Ben Hamper recently quit his day job as a line worker at General Motors. His book *Rivethead* was published by Harper. He lives in Fenton, Michigan, and is working on a second book.

Peter Hannan's cartoon, "The Adventures of a Huge Mouth," have been published in the *Chicago Reader*, *Utne Reader*, *Harpers*, and *Esquire*. He is Associate Art Director for *In These Times*.

Pat Hardin is a cartoonist and illustrator enjoying the urban grit of Flint, Michigan, where he lives with his wife, Shelley Spivack, and their son, Trevor.

Johnny Hart is the creator of the long-running, hit comic strip, "B.C." and the very popular, "Wizard of Id."

What can you say about **Buddy Hickerson** that hasn't been already confessed in court? He's biodegradable, honey-dipped, and gentle to the touch. Vertical when standing, he claims to write and draw the "Quigmans" with the same hand and, while involved in the creative process, enjoys pulling his hair out one by one to get closer to his roots. For reasons unknown he resides in Dallas, Texas.

W. Henri Kreiker, D.E. writes occasionally for the *Journal of Irreproducible Results*. D.E. stands for Distinguished Exterminator.

Garrison Keillor recently returned to St. Paul, Minnesota. He is the long time host of "A Prairie Home Companion" and "The American Radio Company". His most recent book is *We Are Still Married*.

Andrew Lehman - born 12/6/52, Former: Girdle and bra manufacturing plant executive vegetarian restaurant kitchen manager. Present: Co-publishes *Comic Gallery Monthly* and represents alternative cartoonists.

Stan Mack is the creator of "Stan Mack's Real Life Funnies" and can be seen in many publications.

David McCleery is a freelance writer working in Lincoln, Nebraska. He is the owner of A Slow Tempo Press and publishes a monthly magazine of poetry and ideas called *Leaves of Grass*.

Steve McNeon is a cartoonist, animator, and television program developer. He has contributed cartoons to both King Features and United Media. His animation appears on Boston area television as well as PBS, Main Street, and The Learning Channel.

P.S. Mueller's cartoons over the last twenty years have been seen in numerous publications. His books include *Playing Fast and Loose with Time and Space* and *Shrink Wrap*. When not thinking up silly cartoons, he occasionally functions as an editor and writer as well as performing duties with "The Radio Pirates," a cutthroat band of satirists making a name for themselves on public radio. He lives in Madison, Wisconsin, where he is married, has cats, and is a respectable bowler.

Harley Schwadron is a full-time cartoonist living in Ann Arbor, Michigan. His work appears regularly in the *Wall Street Journal* and numerous other publications.

Jim Shahin is the editor of *American Way* magazine. He lives and works in Austin, Texas.

Ian Shoales is the hard-bitten persona of Merle Kessler, a mild-mannered scribbler. Author of *I Gotta Go, Ian Shoales' Perfect World*, and co-author of *The 'Ask Dr. Science' Big Book of Science*. Mr. Kessler was a founding member of Duck's Breath Mystery Theatre, with whom he collaborated on dozens of theatre pieces, radio comedies, films, and television. In the guise of Ian Shoales, he contributes columns to the *San Francisco Examiner* and can be heard on radio stations KCRW in Santa Monica, KQED in San Francisco and NPR's Morning Edition. His commentaries have also appeared in the *New York Times*, among other prestigious or tawdry publications.

Robert Alan Sides, a men's movement leader for 20 years, shrugs in Boston. A member of the Harvard Business School community for 8 years, he now writes/speaks on "men's issues." The first (and so far, only) male alum of Radcliffe College's management program, this neo-'Cliffie represents several national men's groups. Like Malcolm X and Ho Chi Minh, he once worked at the famed Parker house. Some say this makes Robert a revolutionary. Others say, no—just revolting.

Peter Sinclair is the creator of "Alex's Restaurant." His first collection of cartoons was published by The Crossing Press. He lives and works in Midland, Michigan with his wife and two children.

Edward Sorel is the author of *Superpen*. He works in New York City.

Richard Stine lives on an island (which he chooses not to disclose) living a life not unlike his earliest memories: making art, drawing, working in clay, wood, and metal. In addition, he and his wife operate a successful greeting card company, Pal Press. His works have appeared on greeting cards for over 10 years. With the cartoon, "Stine" having appeared in the *Los Angles Herald Examiner*, the *San Francisco Chronicle* and many other publications, Richard's work may be familiar to many of you already.

Mark Stivers attended Tyler School of Art in Philadelphia, where he learned nothing about cartoons. He now lives in Sacramento, California, with his wife, daughter, and two cats.

Charles Varon is a San Francisco humorist known for his intelligent and passionate work on radio, stage, in print, and on bumper stickers. His bumper sticker "Visualize Impeachment" appears to have finally gone out of date.

Brad Veley considers himself a militant feminist trapped inside the body of one of the Three Stooges. "And the worst part" says Veley, "is that it's Shemp, the most boring stooge." As for any profound insights into the Male Human Condition, Veley is at a loss. "Basically," he says, "we are hopeless jerks, and shouldn't be trusted with anything, especially political power, earth moving equipment, or remembering family birthdays." He lives in Marquette, Michigan.

Bob Vojtko, a working class cartoonist, lives with his wife in Lorain, Ohio, on beautiful Lake Erie.

Loudon Wainwright III writes songs from the Westchester Delta Country. His most recent album is *History*. One of his best known songs is "Dead Skunk (in the Middle of the Road)."

Bill Watterson is the creator of "Calvin & Hobbes," one the country's most beloved comic strips. His books have all gone on to be best sellers.

All material in this work is copyright ©1993 by their respective creators unless otherwise noted. No part of this book may be used or reproduced in any manner whatsoever without written permission. Every effort has been made to locate copyright owners and to secure permissions for material used.

Dave Barry's work from *Dave Barry Turns 40*, copyright ©1990 by Dave Barry, reprinted with the permission of Crown Publishers, Inc.

Swami Beyondananda excerpt from *Driving Your Own Karma* by Swami Beyondanada, reprinted with the permission of Destiny Books, an imprint of Inner Traditions International.

Berke Breathed's work copyright © 1986 by Berke Breathed, printed with the permission of The Washington Post Writers' Group.

Joe Bob Briggs excerpt from *Iron Joe Bob*, copyright ©1992 by John Bloom, reprinted with the permission of Atlantic Monthly Press.

Chip Dunham's work from "Overboard," copyright © Universal Press Syndicate, reprinted with permission. All rights reserved.

Gerald Epstein excerpt from *Healing Visualizations*, copyright ©1989 by Gerald Epstein, reprinted with the permission of Bantam Books, a division of Bantam Doubleday Dell Publishing Group, Inc.

"Feiffer" copyright © Jules Feiffer, reprinted with the permission of Universal Press Syndicate. All rights reserved.

Drew and Josh Allan Friedman's work ©1990, reprinted with the permission of Wylie, Aitken & Stone, Inc.

Bud Grace's work reprinted with the permission of King Features Syndicate.

Lewis Grizzard's work from *You Can't Put No Boogie Woogie on the King of Rock and Roll*, copyright ©1991 by Lewis Grizzard, reprinted with the permission of Villard Books, a division of Random House.

Ben Hamper's work reprinted with the permission of David Black Literary Agency.

Johnny Hart's work reprinted with the permission of Johnny Hart and Creators Syndicate, Inc.

Buddy Hickerson's work copyright ©1991, reprinted with the permission of The Los Angeles Times Syndicate.

Garrison Keillor excerpt from *We Are Still Married: Stories and Letters*, copyright © Garrison Keillor, reprinted with the permission of Viking Penguin, a division of Penguin Books USA, Inc.

Barry A. Scherr's work from *The Best of the Journal of Irreproducible Results*, copyright ©1983 by the *Journal of Irreproducible Results* and Barry A Scherr, reprinted with the permission of Workman Publishing Company, Inc. All rights reserved.

Edward Sorel's work from *Superpen* copyright ©1978 by Edward Sorel, reprinted with the permission of Random House, Inc.

Mark Twain excerpt reprinted with the permission of the Mark Twain Foundation.

Loudon Wainright, copyright © Loudon Wainright III, reprinted with the permision of Snowden Music Inc.

Bill Watterson's work from "Calvin and Hobbes," copyright ©1993, reprinted with the permission of Universal Press Syndicate. All rights reserved.

**Add more humor books to your collection
from The Crossing Press.
To receive our current catalog, please call
Toll Free 1-800-777-1048**